Pizza
For Every Meal & Occasion

Printed in the United States of America
by G&R Publishing Co.

Distributed By:

Products

507 Industrial Street
Waverly, IA 50677

ISBN-13: 978-1-56383-221-5
ISBN-10: 1-56383-221-6
Item #7013

Table
of
Contents

Breakfast Pizza.............................. 1-12

Appetizer Party Pizza 13-28

Main Dish Pizza 29-62

Pizza for One............................... 63-78

Crusts and Sauces 79-100

Dessert Pizza............................ 101-118

Index 119-121

Pizza, Pizza, Pizza!

Millions of pizzas are consumed daily all around the world. In America, pizza, by far, has become the country's favorite food over the past 50 years. Pizza is served in homes, restaurants, schools and gas stations across the United States. It is both fast food and gourmet. Pizza now comes in many shapes and sizes and has been topped with just about any ingredient imaginable. This American Pie is often the perfect dish for just about every meal and occasion. Within this book, discover pizza recipes for breakfast, lunch, dinner, dessert, appetizers, parties and personal pizza made just for one! Whether it's traditional, thin crust, deep dish, wrapped as a calzone or spread over a pita – find your favorite recipe and enjoy the aromas, the taste and the joy of creating pizza in your own home!

Pizza Tips

- The best way to layer a pizza is by starting with the crust, followed by the sauce, then cheese and, finally, the toppings.

- If making homemade dough, follow directions carefully and precisely. Moist dough will make a tender crust.

- Baking pizzas on pizza stones provides a uniformly heated surface that absorbs moisture from the crust, resulting in a crisper crust.

- Use pizza stones on the lowest rack in your oven and preheat the stone in the oven.

- Cut the pizza with the largest pizza cutter available and cut fast, so the cheese and toppings will not stick to the cutter.

- Dust unused dough with flour and place in a ziplock back. Store in the refrigerator for up to 1 week.

- Add a kick to homemade sauce by adding a little balsamic vinegar to the recipe.

- Try various cheeses and cheese blends. Whole milk mozzarella cheese melts smoothly and has a rich taste.

- Thoroughly drain any toppings that would add moisture or sogginess to the pizza, such as packaged olives, artichoke hearts or anchovies.

- Rub dry herbs between fingers as they are sprinkled over the pizza. This will release the oils and flavor of the herbs.

- Let baked pizza cool on a wire rack for 2 to 3 minutes before cutting.

Breakfast Pizza

Sausage & Egg Breakfast Pizza

Makes 2 (12") pizzas

2 (12") pre-baked pizza
  crusts
1/2 lb. pork sausage
1/2 lb. Italian sausage
2 cloves garlic, minced
Black pepper, to taste
1 lb. bacon

5 eggs, beaten
Olive oil
1 (12 oz.) jar nacho
  cheese sauce
2 C. shredded mozzarella
  cheese

Preheat oven to 450°. Grease or line 2 pizza pans with parchment baking paper, trimming so the paper does not hang over the edge of the pan. Place one pizza crust on each lined pan. In a large skillet over medium heat, heat pork sausage, Italian sausage and minced garlic until cooked throughout. Remove from skillet, drain well and crumble. Add pepper to taste. In the same large skillet, cook bacon until well done, drain and crumble. Clean skillet and cook beaten eggs until soft scrambled. Drizzle olive oil over pizza crusts. Pour an even amount of nacho cheese sauce over each crust. Layer the remaining ingredients over the crusts, beginning with the cooked sausage, scrambled eggs, half of the mozzarella cheese, half of the bacon and top with remaining cheese. Crumble remaining bacon over pizzas. Reduce oven temperature to 425° and bake, one pizza at a time, for 12 minutes. For a crisper crust, place the pizza directly on the oven rack and bake for an additional 3 minutes. Repeat with second pizza.

Gourmet Smoked Salmon Breakfast Pizza

Makes 1 (10") pizza

1 (10") focaccia bread, flat bread or cooked pizza crust
8 eggs
1/4 C. plain yogurt or sour cream
2 T. fresh dillweed
2 T. chopped green onions

2 T. fresh chopped parsley
1/4 tsp. pepper
2 T. butter
6 oz. thinly sliced smoked salmon
Additional pepper, green onions or dillweed, to taste

Preheat oven to 350°. If focaccia bread is thicker than 1", cut in half horizontally. Warm the bread or crust in oven for 10 minutes. In a large mixing bowl, whisk together eggs, yogurt, dillweed, green onions, parsley and pepper until well mixed. In a large skillet over medium heat, melt butter. Add the egg mixture and stir gently so mixture stays moist. Spoon cooked eggs onto the warmed crust. Place slices of smoked salmon over the eggs. Sprinkle with additional seasonings to taste.

Beginning in 1987, October was named National Pizza Month.

3

Egg & Ham Biscuit Pizzas

Makes 6 (5") pizzas

3 bell peppers, any color, sliced thin
1 onion, sliced thin
1 C. cooked, diced ham
2 C. flour
1 tsp. baking powder
1 tsp. salt
1/2 C. cold butter, cut into pieces
10 T. milk
2 C. shredded Cheddar cheese
6 eggs

Preheat oven to 425°. In a large skillet, cook peppers and onion until softened. Add cooked ham and remove from heat. To make dough, in a large bowl, combine flour, baking powder and salt. Cut in butter and mix well. When mixture resembles course meal, add milk and mix until it forms a soft dough. Shape dough into a ball and knead 6 times on a lightly floured, flat surface. Cut dough into 6 pieces. Roll each piece into a 7" circle, making a 1/2" rim on each by pinching up the edge. Circles should measure 5" when complete. Place biscuits on large greased baking sheets. Top each biscuit with Cheddar cheese and some of the ham mixture. Make an indentation in the center of each biscuit. Crack and drop one egg into the indentation in each biscuit. Bake in oven for 12 to 15 minutes, or until eggs are set.

Pizza Omelet

Makes 2 omelets

3 eggs
2 T. water
1 T. butter
3 T. pizza sauce
1/2 C. shredded
   mozzarella cheese

Salt and pepper, to taste
Pepperoni slices, optional
Mushroom slices, optional
Diced green peppers,
   optional
Diced onions, optional

In a large mixing bowl, whisk together eggs and water. In a large skillet over medium heat, melt butter. Pour egg mixture into hot skillet. When eggs are nearly set, spread pizza sauce over the eggs. Top with cheese and add any additional ingredients you desire. Cover skillet and remove from heat. Let stand for about 2 minutes. Cut in half to make 2 omelets.

Each year, pizza is a $30 billion industry.

Breakfast Pizza Casserole

Makes 6 servings

1 (10 oz.) can refrigerated biscuits
1 (11 oz.) pkg. frozen scalloped potatoes, thawed
4 eggs, lightly beaten
1 C. shredded Cheddar cheese, divided
1/2 tsp. onion powder
1/8 tsp. pepper
1 lb. ground sausage, cooked, drained and crumbled
1 (8 oz.) jar salsa, optional

Preheat oven to 400°. In a 9x13" baking dish, press biscuits to form a 1/8" bottom layer. Bake in oven for 6 to 7 minutes, until lightly browned. In a medium mixing bowl, combine potatoes, eggs, half of the cheese, onion powder and pepper. Spread mixture over biscuits and top with cooked sausage and remaining cheese. Bake in oven until a knife inserted in center of casserole comes out clean, approximately 25 to 30 minutes. If desired, top with salsa. To serve, cut into squares.

Croissant Sausage Breakfast Pizza

Makes 2 (12") pizzas

2 (8 1/2 oz.) cans
  refrigerated
  crescent rolls
2 (16 oz.) pkgs. pork
  sausage, cooked,
  crumbled and drained
2 C. frozen hash brown
  potato cubes, thawed
1/3 C. diced green bell
  pepper, optional
1/3 C. diced red bell
  pepper, optional

1/3 C. diced yellow bell
  pepper, optional
1/2 C. thinly sliced green
  onions, optional
2 C. shredded sharp
  Cheddar cheese
6 eggs, lightly beaten
1/3 C. milk
1 tsp. salt
2 tsp. pepper
1/4 C. grated Parmesan
  cheese

Preheat oven to 375°. Separate crescent rolls into individual sections. Divide sections, with points toward the center, onto 2 ungreased 12" pizza pans. Press together, sealing crescent rolls to form a circle 1" larger than each pizza pan. Turn edges under to make a 1" rim. Sprinkle sausage and potatoes over crust in both pizza pans. If desired, add peppers and onions. Sprinkle with Cheddar cheese. In a small mixing bowl, combine eggs, milk, salt and pepper, stirring well. Divide evenly and pour mixture over each pizza. Sprinkle with Parmesan cheese. Bake in oven for 15 to 20 minutes, or until eggs are set and crust is golden brown.

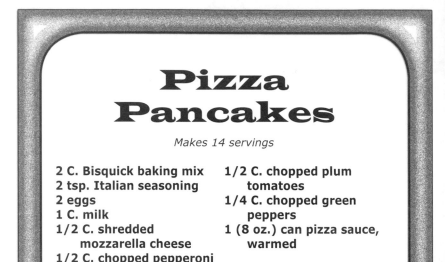

Pizza Pancakes

Makes 14 servings

2 C. Bisquick baking mix
2 tsp. Italian seasoning
2 eggs
1 C. milk
1/2 C. shredded
  mozzarella cheese
1/2 C. chopped pepperoni

1/2 C. chopped plum
  tomatoes
1/4 C. chopped green
  peppers
1 (8 oz.) can pizza sauce,
  warmed

In a large bowl, combine baking mix and Italian seasoning. In a separate bowl, whisk together eggs and milk. Add milk mixture to dry ingredients, stirring just until moistened. Fold in shredded mozzarella cheese, chopped pepperoni, chopped tomatoes and chopped green peppers. To make pancakes, in a medium skillet over medium high heat, place a thin layer of grease. Pour 1/4 cup of the batter mixture into the hot skillet and cook until bubbles appear on the top surface of the pancake. Carefully flip over pancake until golden brown on both sides. Remove pancake from skillet and repeat with remaining batter. Serve with warmed pizza sauce on the side.

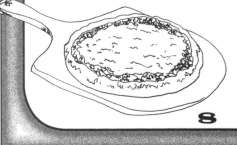

Cheesy Tomato & Mushroom Breakfast Pizza

Makes 6 to 8 servings

1 lb. ground pork sausage
1 (8 oz.) can refrigerated
   crescent rolls
1 (10 oz.) can diced
   tomatoes with green
   chile peppers, drained
1 (6 oz.) can mushroom
   pieces, drained

1 C. shredded Cheddar
   cheese, divided
1 C. shredded mozzarella
   cheese, divided
6 eggs
1 tsp. Worcestershire
   sauce
Salt and pepper, to taste

Preheat oven to 350°. In a large skillet over medium heat, cook sausage until evenly browned. Drain, crumble and set aside. Line bottom and sides of a 9x13" baking dish with crescent rolls. Top with cooked sausage, drained tomatoes, drained mushrooms, half of the Cheddar cheese and half of the mozzarella cheese. Bake in oven for 8 to 10 minutes, or until crust is golden brown. Remove from oven and set aside. In a large mixing bowl, beat together eggs, Worcestershire sauce, salt and pepper. Pour mixture over crust and bake for an additional 7 to 9 minutes, or until eggs are set. Remove from oven and top with remaining cheese.

Double Sausage Breakfast Pie

Makes 2 (12") pizzas

2 (12") unbaked pizza crusts

1 lb. Italian sausage, cooked

1 (12 oz.) jar spicy pizza sauce

1 1/2 C. shredded mozzarella cheese

1 lb. smoked sausage links, cooked

1 1/2 C. shredded Monterey Jack chees

Preheat oven to 400°. Place pizza crusts on baking pans. In a medium bowl, combine Italian sausage and pizza sauce. Mix well and spread over crusts. Cover each pizza with mozzarella cheese and place precooked sausage links in a circular pattern on top. Sprinkle with Monterey Jack cheese. Bake pizzas in oven for 15 minutes.

Americans consume about 251,770,000 pounds of pepperoni each year!

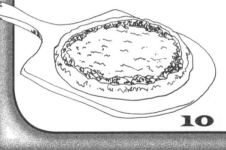

10

Sweet Apple Cheddar Breakfast Pizza

Makes 2 (12") pizzas

8 medium Golden
Delicious apples
3 T. butter
1 C. brown sugar
3 T. cinnamon
1 T. nutmeg
1 T. allspice

1 lb. pork sausage
2 (12") pre-baked pizza
crusts
3 1/2 C. shredded
Cheddar cheese,
divided

Preheat oven to 400°. Peel and slice the apples. In a large skillet over medium heat, melt butter. Add sliced apples and cover skillet. Cook for 8 minutes, stirring occasionally, until apples are tender. Stir in brown sugar, cinnamon, nutmeg and allspice and continue to cook for 2 minutes, or until apples are glazed. In another large skillet, cook sausage until heated throughout and drain. Divide all ingredients in half evenly. Cover each crust with 1 1/2 cups Cheddar cheese and spread with baked apples. Bake in oven for 5 minutes. Top with cooked sausage and remaining cheese and bake for an additional 5 minutes.

Ricotta Pizza Quiche

Makes 6 to 8 servings

1/2 lb. Italian sausage	1 (3 1/2 oz.) pkg. sliced
1 (9") double crust pastry	pepperoni, chopped
3 eggs, lightly beaten	1/2 C. grated Parmesan
1 C. ricotta cheese	cheese
1 tsp. Italian seasoning	3/4 C. pizza sauce
1 C. shredded mozzarella	
cheese	

Preheat oven to 450°. In a medium skillet over medium heat, brown sausage, drain, crumble and set aside. Line a 9" pie plate or quiche dish with one of the pie crusts and flute the edge. Bake in oven for 5 minutes, prick crust with a fork and bake for an additional 5 minutes. Remove from oven and reduce oven temperature to 350°. In a large mixing bowl, combine eggs, ricotta cheese and Italian seasoning, mixing well. Stir in cooked sausage, mozzarella cheese, chopped pepperoni and Parmesan cheese. Pour mixture into baked pie crust. Cut remaining pie crust into an 8" circle and slice circle into 6 wedges. Arrange wedges over quiche filling. Bake in oven for 45 to 50 minutes, or until golden brown. Remove from oven and let cool for 10 minutes. Spoon pizza sauce over each pastry wedge.

Appetizer Party Pizza

No-Bake Chicken Veggie Pizza

Makes 1 (12") pizza

1 C. prepared spinach dip
1 (12") pre-baked pizza
   crust
1 C. chopped broccoli
1 C. cooked, cubed
   chicken

1/3 C. chopped green
   onions
1 medium tomato,
   chopped

Spread spinach dip to within 1/2" of the edge of pizza crust. Top pizza evenly with chopped broccoli, cubed chicken, chopped green onions and chopped tomato. Cut pizza into wedges and serve.

Pizza Roll-Ups

Makes 10 servings

1 (10 oz.) can
   refrigerated
   pizza crust dough
1/4 lb. sliced salami
1/4 lb. sliced pepperoni

1/4 lb. sliced provolone
   cheese
1/2 C. shredded
   mozzarella cheese

Preheat oven to 350°. Lightly grease a baking sheet. Roll out pizza crust dough to a 10x14" rectangle and place on the prepared baking sheet. Evenly layer pizza with sliced salami, sliced pepperoni and sliced provolone cheese. Sprinkle the top of the pizza with mozzarella cheese to within 1/2" of the edge. Roll pizza, jelly roll style, starting at the short end, and seal the edges. Bake in oven for 25 minutes, or until golden brown. Slice pizza roll into 1" pieces and serve.

In America, we consume about 350 slices of pizza each second!

Veggie Pizza Bites

Makes 24 servings

2 (8 oz.) cans
  refrigerated
  crescent rolls
1 (6 oz.) tub whipped
  extra sharp
  Cheddar cheese

1/2 C. sour cream
1 1/2 tsp. dillweed
1 tsp. onion salt
5 C. chopped assorted
  fresh vegetables

Preheat oven to 375°. Line a 10x15" baking dish with aluminum foil. Press all of the crescent rolls evenly into the bottom of the prepared dish. Bake in oven for 11 to 13 minutes, or until golden brown. Remove from oven and let cool. In a large bowl, combine whipped cheese, sour cream, dillweed and onion salt, mixing until well blended. Spread mixture evenly over cooled crust. Top with assorted vegetables and, if desired, sprinkle with additional dillweed. Cut into squares or triangles and serve.

Party Pizzas on Rye

Makes 15 servings

1 lb. ground beef
1 lb. ground spicy
   pork sausage
1/2 C. cubed processed
   American cheese

Dash of hot pepper sauce
1 (16 oz.) pkg. cocktail
   rye bread

Preheat oven to 375°. In a large skillet over medium heat, combine ground beef and ground sausage. Heat until cooked throughout and evenly browned. Drain skillet of fat. Add cubed cheese to browned meat mixture. Cook over low heat until cheese melts, stirring frequently. Add hot pepper sauce to desired taste. Spread a layer of the cheesy meat mixture over each rye bread slice. Place the prepared rye slices on an ungreased baking sheet. Bake in oven for 15 to 20 minutes, or until topping is lightly browned. Serve warm.

In America, we consume about 100 acres of pizza per day!

Three Cheese Pizza Wedges

Makes 24 servings

1 (12") pre-baked pizza crust

2 cloves garlic, minced, divided

1 T. butter or margarine, melted

1 (8 oz.) pkg. cream cheese, softened

1 (8 oz.) pkg. shredded pizza blend cheese

1/4 C. grated Parmesan cheese

1/2 tsp. dried oregano

1 C. pizza sauce, warm

Preheat oven to 400°. Place the pizza crust on a large baking sheet or 12" pizza pan. In a medium bowl, combine half of the minced garlic and the melted butter. Mix well and brush evenly over pizza crust. In a separate medium bowl, combine softened cream cheese, shredded pizza blend cheese, grated Parmesan cheese, oregano and remaining minced garlic, stirring until well blended. Spread cheese mixture evenly over pizza crust. Bake in oven 10 to 12 minutes, or until cheese is melted and crust is golden brown. Cut pizza into 24 wedges and serve with warm pizza sauce for dipping.

Broccoli Ranch Veggie Pizza

Makes 1 (12") pizza

2 (8 oz.) cans
   refrigerated
   crescent rolls
1 (8 oz.) pkg. cream
   cheese, softened
1 (1 oz.) pkg. dry ranch
   dressing mix

1/2 C. mayonnaise
2 C. chopped broccoli
1/2 C. chopped
   cauliflower
2 C. shredded Cheddar
   cheese

Preheat oven to 375°. Press all of the crescent rolls evenly into the bottom of a 12" pizza pan. Bake in oven for 8 minutes, or until crust is lightly browned. In a medium bowl, combine softened cream cheese, ranch dressing mix and mayonnaise, stirring until well blended. Remove crust from oven and let cool. Spread the cream cheese mixture evenly over the cooled pizza crust. Top pizza with chopped broccoli, chopped cauliflower and shredded Cheddar cheese. Cut into wedges and serve.

Throughout the United States, there are approximately 61,269 pizza parlors.

19

Gelatin Fruit Pizza

Makes 1 (12") pizza

1 (8 oz.) pkg. gelatin, any flavor	2 C. fresh chopped fruit
2 1/2 C. boiling water	1 C. whipped topping

Grease a 12" deep-dish pizza pan with non-stick cooking spray. In a medium bowl or saucepan, combine gelatin and boiling water, stirring until gelatin is completely dissolved. Stir in fresh chopped fruit and pour mixture into prepared pan. Chill in refrigerator until gelatin is firm. Top with an even layer of whipped topping. Cut into squares and serve.

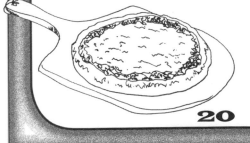

Cheese-Stuffed Pizza Puffs

Makes 10 servings

**4 to 6 oz. mozzarella
  cheese
1 (8 oz.) can
  refrigerated
  buttermilk biscuits**

**1/4 C. pizza sauce
Grated Parmesan cheese
Dried oregano**

Preheat oven to 425°. Cut mozzarella cheese into 10 cubes. Press 1 cube of cheese into each biscuit and pinch to seal the cheese on the inside. On an ungreased baking sheet, place biscuits, pinched seams down. Top each biscuit with approximately 1 teaspoon pizza sauce, spreading evenly over each biscuit. Sprinkle with desired amount of Parmesan cheese and dried oregano. Bake in oven for 15 minutes, or until golden brown. Serve immediately.

Easy Pizza Logs

Makes 4 servings

1/2 C. pizza sauce, divided	1/2 C. shredded mozzarella cheese
4 (8") tortillas	Pizza toppings, optional

Preheat oven to 200°. Spread 2 tablespoons pizza sauce evenly over each tortilla. Sprinkle 2 tablespoons mozzarella cheese over sauce on each tortilla and add additional pizza toppings, if desired. Roll up tortillas and place on a baking sheet, seam side down. Bake in oven for 5 to 10 minutes, until tortillas are warmed. If desired, cut into 1" slices and secure each slice with a toothpick before serving.

Pepperoni is the topping of choice for approximately 36% of all pizzas ordered.

Apple Pizza Pie

Makes 8 to 10 servings

1/2 tsp. sugar
1/2 C. warm water
11/2 tsp. active dry yeast
1 T. butter, melted and
  cooled
1 1/2 C. flour, divided
Pinch of salt
6 C. sliced apples
2 T. lemon juice

1/2 C. brown sugar
1 1/4 tsp. cinnamon
1/4 C. butter, softened
1/2 C. breadcrumbs
1 C. shredded Cheddar
  cheese
1 C. shredded mozzarella
  cheese

Preheat oven to 450°. To prepare pizza dough, in a large bowl, dissolve sugar in warm water. Sprinkle yeast over water mixture and let stand 10 minutes, or until water is foamy. Stir in melted butter, 3/4 cup flour and a pinch of salt. Gradually stir in the remaining flour, until mixture forms a sticky ball of dough. On a lightly floured flat surface, knead dough for 5 minutes, or until smooth. Place dough in a large greased bowl. Cover bowl with a kitchen towel and let stand for 15 minutes. Punch down dough and roll out into a 15" circle. Place dough on a greased 12" pizza pan and set aside. In a medium bowl, place sliced apples. Sprinkle apples with lemon juice. Arrange apples over pizza crust and sprinkle with brown sugar and cinnamon. In a separate bowl, place dry breadcrumbs. Using a pastry blender, cut in softened butter and sprinkle mixture over apples. Top pizza with shredded Cheddar cheese and shredded mozzarella cheese. Bake in oven for 20 minutes, or until golden brown. Cut into wedges and serve warm.

Brie Pecan Party Pizza

Makes 8 servings

1 (8 oz.) can
   refrigerated
   crescent rolls
1 C. cubed Brie cheese

3/4 C. cranberry sauce
   or raspberry jam
1/2 C. chopped pecans

Preheat oven to 425°. Grease a 12" pizza pan or 9x13" baking dish. Separate crescent rolls into individual pieces. Lightly press crescent rolls, with tips towards the center, into the prepared pan. Bake in oven for 5 minutes, or until lightly browned. Remove crust from the oven and sprinkle with Brie cheese cubes. Spread cranberry sauce over the cubed cheese and sprinkle with chopped pecans. Return to oven for an additional 8 minutes, or until cheese is melted and crust is golden brown. Remove from oven and let cool for 5 minutes. Cut into squares and serve.

Sugar Cookie Fruit Pizza

Makes 1 pizza

1 (18 oz.) pkg.
   refrigerated sugar
   cookie dough
1 (7 oz.) jar
   marshmallow cream

1 (8 oz.) pkg. cream
   cheese, softened
2 C. various fresh
   chopped fruits

Preheat oven to 350°. On an ungreased baking sheet, form the sugar cookie dough evenly into a 1/4" crust. Bake in oven for 10 minutes, or until edges are browned and center is no longer doughy. In a medium bowl, combine marshmallow cream and softened cream cheese, blending until smooth. Spread the mixture evenly over the sugar cookie crust. Top pizza with various fresh chopped fruits, such as strawberries, kiwis, grapes or blueberries. Refrigerate until ready to serve. Before serving, cut into squares.

According to the Gallup Poll, children ages 3 to 11 prefer pizza over all other foods for lunch and dinner.

Italian Pizza Roll Bread

Makes 14 to 20 servings

4 C. flour
1 tsp. salt
1 T. active dry yeast
1 1/3 C. warm water
2 T. vegetable oil
1 T. sugar
1 1/2 lb. Italian sausage
1 (12 oz.) can tomato paste

3 T. minced onion
2 tsp. minced garlic
2 tsp. dried oregano
2/3 C. grated Romano cheese
1 1/2 C. shredded mozzarella cheese
2 T. olive oil

Preheat oven to 400°. In a large mixing bowl, combine flour and salt. Form a well in the center of the flour mixture and add yeast, water, oil and sugar. Let stand for 5 minutes, or until yeast dissolves and starts to foam. Stir with a spoon until a soft dough forms. On a lightly floured flat surface, knead dough until smooth, adding more flour as needed. Cover bowl with a kitchen towel and let stand for 15 minutes. Punch down dough and divide in half. Meanwhile, in a large skillet over medium heat, cook sausage until heated throughout and drain of fat. Stir in tomato paste, minced onion, minced garlic and oregano. Remove from heat and let cool. Form each half of dough into a 9x14" rectangle. Divide sausage mixture in half and spread over each crust to within 1/2" of the edge. Sprinkle pizzas with grated Romano cheese and shredded mozzarella cheese and drizzle with olive oil. Roll pizzas, jelly roll style, starting at the long end, and seal the edges. Bend each pizza roll into a crescent shape and place on greased baking sheets. Bake in oven for 45 minutes, or until golden brown. Remove from oven and let cool for 30 minutes before cutting into 2" to 3" slices.

Hot Dog Pizza

Makes 1 (12") pizza

1/2 C. pizza sauce
1 T. ketchup
1 tsp. prepared mustard
1 (12") pre-baked pizza
   crust

1 (16 oz.) pkg. hot dogs
1 (8 oz.) pkg. shredded
   pizza blend cheese

Preheat oven to 400°. In a medium bowl, combine pizza sauce, ketchup and mustard. Spread mixture evenly over pre-baked pizza crust. Slice hot dogs into 1/4" pieces. Arrange hot dogs evenly over sauce mixture. Sprinkle shredded pizza blend cheese over pizza. Place the pizza on an ungreased baking sheet. Bake in oven for 10 to 15 minutes, or until crust is brown and cheese is melted. Cut into wedges and serve.

Three billion pizzas are sold every year in the United States.

27

Strawberry Almond Pizza

Make 1 (12") pizza

3/4 C. almonds
1/2 C. plus 1 T. sugar, divided
1 (12") pre-baked pizza crust
6 T. butter, softened
1 egg, lightly beaten
1 T. raspberry liqueur, optional

1/2 tsp. almond extract
16 oz. sliced fresh strawberries
1/4 C. raspberry jam, melted
Whipped topping
Sliced toasted almonds

Preheat oven to 400°. In a blender or food processor, combine almonds and 1 tablespoon sugar. Process until ground. Place pizza crust on a 12" pan lined with parchment paper. In a medium bowl, cream together softened butter and remaining 1/2 cup sugar. Stir in egg, raspberry liqueur and almond extract, mixing well. Stir in ground almonds mixture. Spread creamed mixture evenly over the pizza crust. Bake in oven for 15 to 20 minutes, or until topping is golden brown. Remove from oven and let cool. Arrange sliced strawberries over pizza and brush with melted raspberry jam. If desired, garnish with whipped topping and sliced almonds. Cut into squares and serve.

Main Dish Pizza

BLT Pizza

Makes 1 (12") pizza

1 (12") pre-baked pizza
   crust
8 slices bacon, crisp
   cooked
4 tomatoes, chopped

5 T. mayonnaise
1 small lettuce head,
   shredded, divided
Salt and pepper, to taste

Preheat oven to 425°. Crumble crisp cooked bacon into pieces. In a large bowl, combine crumbled bacon, chopped tomatoes, mayonnaise and half of the shredded lettuce. Add salt and pepper to taste. Spread mixture over pre-baked pizza crust. Bake in oven for 20 minutes. Remove from oven and top with additional shredded lettuce. Cut into slices and serve immediately.

Americans eat, on average, about 23 pounds of pizza every year.

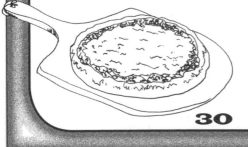

Thai Chicken & Shrimp Pizza

Makes 1 (12") pizza

3 boneless, skinless chicken breasts
1 to 2 T. peanut oil
1 1/3 C. peanut sauce, divided
1/3 lb. uncooked shrimp, peeled and de-veined
1 (12") pre-baked pizza crust
3/4 C. shredded mozzarella cheese
1/2 C. shredded Swiss cheese
4 green onions, sliced
1 carrot, cut into long thin strips
1/2 C. chopped peanuts
1/3 C. fresh chopped cilantro

Preheat oven to 400°. To prepare chicken, in a large skillet over medium heat, sauté chicken breasts in peanut oil until lightly browned on both sides. Remove from skillet and cut into small cubes. Pour 1/2 cup peanut sauce in heated skillet and return cubed chicken to skillet. Cook and toss until evenly coated. Remove chicken from skillet and set aside. To prepare shrimp, in the same skillet over medium heat, sauté shrimp until pink, about 3 minutes. Remove shrimp from skillet and chop into desired size pieces. Add 1/2 cup peanut sauce to hot skillet and return chopped shrimp to skillet. Heat and toss until evenly coated. Spread remaining 1/3 cup peanut sauce over pre-baked pizza crust. Sprinkle shredded mozzarella cheese and Swiss cheese over pizza to within 1/2" of the edge. Spoon coated chicken and shrimp pieces evenly over the cheese and top with sliced green onions, sliced carrots and chopped peanuts. Bake in oven for 10 to 15 minutes, or until crust is golden brown. Remove pizza from oven and sprinkle with fresh chopped cilantro. Let cool for 10 minutes before cutting into slices.

Chicken Caesar Salad Pizza

Makes 1 (12") pizza

2 boneless, skinless
   chicken breasts
2 cloves garlic, minced
1 small onion, chopped
1 red bell pepper,
   chopped
Caesar salad dressing
1 (10 oz.) can
   refrigerated pizza
   crust dough

1 C. shredded mozzarella
   cheese
1/4 C. grated Parmesan
   cheese
1/2 head Romaine
   lettuce, shredded
2 tomatoes, diced
Croutons, optional

Preheat oven to 350°. Chop chicken breasts into 1" pieces. In a large skillet over medium heat, cook chicken pieces until heated throughout and no longer pink. Remove cooked chicken pieces and set aside. In a separate large skillet over medium heat, combine minced garlic, chopped onion, chopped red bell pepper and 2 tablespoons Caesar salad dressing, sautéing until tender. Add cooked chicken and heat, mixing well, for 1 additional minute. Spread pizza crust dough evenly over a 12" pizza pan or over a baking stone, pinching the edge to form a ridge. Lightly brush pizza crust with additional Caesar salad dressing. Spread chicken mixture evenly over the crust and sprinkle with shredded mozzarella cheese and grated Parmesan cheese. Bake in oven for 20 to 25 minutes, or until crust is golden brown and cheese is melted. In a medium bowl, toss shredded Romaine lettuce with diced tomatoes and desired amount of Caesar salad dressing. Remove pizza from oven and top with lettuce mixture. If desired, sprinkle croutons over pizza. Cut into slices and serve warm.

Smoked Salmon Pizza

Makes 1 (12") pizza

1 (12") unbaked pizza crust
1 (4 oz.) pkg. cream cheese, softened
1/4 C. minced red onion
1 T. fresh dillweed

2 tsp. grated lemon peel
1 tsp. prepared horseradish
Salt and pepper, to taste
Thinly sliced smoked salmon

Preheat oven to 450°. On a large baking sheet, place pizza crust and bake in oven for about 13 minutes, or until edges are crisp. Remove from oven and let cool until just warm. In a medium bowl, combine softened cream cheese, minced red onion, dillweed, grated lemon peel and horseradish, stirring until well mixed. Add salt and pepper to taste. Spread cream cheese mixture over warm crust to within 1" of the edge. Top pizza with desired amount of sliced smoked salmon. Cut into slices and serve.

Some popular pizza toppings in Japan are squid and Mayo Jaga, a combination of mayonnaise, potato and bacon.

33

Zucchini Crust Pizza

Makes 1 (11x15") pizza

4 C. peeled and
   shredded zucchini
2 C. cooked rice
1 1/2 C. shredded
   mozzarella cheese
1 C. grated Parmesan
   cheese
2 eggs, lightly beaten

1 lb. cooked ground beef
1 medium onion, chopped
1 1/2 C. spaghetti sauce
1 tsp. dried oregano
1/2 tsp. salt
2 C. shredded Cheddar
   cheese

Preheat oven to 400°. In a large bowl, combine shredded zucchini, cooked rice, shredded mozzarella cheese, grated Parmesan cheese and eggs. Mix until well combined. Grease a 11X15" jellyroll pan and press zucchini mixture evenly into bottom of pan. Bake in oven for 20 to 25 minutes, or until golden brown. Meanwhile, in a medium bowl, combine browned ground beef, chopped onion, spaghetti sauce, dried oregano and salt, mixing well. Spread ground beef mixture evenly over layer in pan and sprinkle with shredded Cheddar cheese. Return to oven for an additional 15 minutes. Remove from oven and let stand 5 minutes before cutting into slices.

Herbed White Pizza

Makes 1 (12") pizza

1 T. olive oil
1 clove garlic, minced
1 (12") pre-baked pizza
   crust
3/4 C. shredded
   mozzarella cheese

2 tsp. grated Parmesan
   cheese
1 tsp. fresh chopped
   parsley
1/8 tsp. dried oregano
3/4 C. cottage cheese

Preheat oven to 400°. In a small skillet over medium heat, sauté minced garlic in olive oil until garlic is golden brown. Brush garlic mixture evenly over pre-baked crust to within 1/2" of the edge. Sprinkle shredded mozzarella cheese over crust and bake in oven for 10 minutes. Meanwhile, in a small bowl, combine grated Parmesan cheese, fresh chopped parsley and dried oregano. Mix well and set aside. Remove pizza from oven and spread cottage cheese in an even layer over pizza. Sprinkle Parmesan cheese mixture over cottage cheese. Return to oven for an additional 10 to 15 minutes. Remove from oven and let cool slightly before cutting into slices.

The pizza topping of choice in Brazil is green peas.

Garlic Veggie Chicken Pizza

Makes 1 (12") pizza

1 (4 oz.) pkg. cream
   cheese, softened
1/4 C. sour cream
2 cloves garlic, mashed
1 (12") pre-baked pizza
   crust
1 C. cooked, diced
   chicken
1/2 C. chopped red
   onions

1/2 tomato, chopped
1/2 C. chopped red
   bell peppers
1/2 C. sliced mushrooms
1 C. shredded
   mozzarella cheese
3 T. grated Parmesan
   cheese

Preheat oven to 350°. In a large bowl, combine softened cream cheese, sour cream and mashed garlic, mixing until smooth. Spread cream cheese mixture evenly over pre-baked pizza crust. Cover with cooked chicken, chopped red onions, chopped tomato, chopped red bell pepper, sliced mushrooms and shredded mozzarella cheese. Bake in oven for 15 minutes, or until crust is golden brown and cheese is melted. Remove from oven and sprinkle with grated Parmesan cheese. Cut into slices and serve immediately.

Fajita Pizza

Makes 1 (12") pizza

1 (12") pre-baked
   pizza crust
Olive oil
1 medium green bell
   pepper, sliced
1 medium red bell
   pepper, sliced
1 medium onion, sliced
2 chicken breast halves

2 tsp. fajita seasoning
1 clove garlic, minced
1/4 C. chunky salsa
2 C. shredded Colby
   and Monterey Jack
   cheese blend, divided
2 T. fresh chopped cilantro
Sour cream, if desired

Preheat oven to 450°. Place pre-baked pizza crust on a lightly greased 12" pizza pan. Using a pastry brush, brush olive oil over crust. In a large skillet over medium heat, place an additional 1/2 teaspoon olive oil. Slice bell peppers and onions into 1/2" strips and slice the chicken breast halves into thin strips. Place sliced chicken in heated skillet and sauté until chicken is no longer pink. Add another 1/2 teaspoon olive oil, sliced red peppers, sliced green peppers, sliced onions, fajita seasoning and minced garlic. Sauté mixture until chicken is cooked throughout and vegetables are tender. Remove from heat and drain off fat. Stir in chunky salsa. Reduce oven temperature to 425°. Sprinkle 1 cup shredded cheese blend over pizza crust and spread chicken mixture over the cheese. Top with remaining 1 cup cheese blend. Bake in oven for 12 minutes. For a crisper crust, remove pizza from pan and place pizza directly on oven rack for an additional 3 minutes. Remove pizza from oven and garnish with fresh chopped cilantro. Let cool 5 minutes before cutting into slices. If desired, serve with sour cream on the side.

Simple Artichoke Pesto Pizza

Makes 1 (12") pizza

Olive oil
1 (12") pre-baked
   pizza crust
1 C. prepared pesto
   sauce
1 C. chopped artichoke
   hearts
1 C. chopped sun-dried
   tomatoes
1 C. spinach leaves
1/2 C. whole green olives

1/2 C. crumbled feta
   cheese
1/2 C. shredded
   mozzarella cheese
Pine nuts, optional
Chicken breast strips,
   optional
Fresh basil, optional
Bell peppers, optional
Pepperoni or salami,
   optional

Preheat oven to 350˚. Using a pastry brush, brush olive oil over pre-baked pizza crust. Spread pesto sauce evenly over pizza crust. Top with chopped artichoke hearts, chopped sun-dried tomatoes, spinach leaves and green olives. Sprinkle crumbled feta cheese and shredded mozzarella cheese over pizza. If desired, pizza can be topped with pine nuts, chicken strips, basil, bell peppers or pepperoni. Place pizza directly on oven rack and bake for 10 minutes, or until cheese is melted. Remove from oven and let cool for 5 minutes before cutting into slices.

Feta, Onions & Spinach Pizza

Makes 1 (10") pizza

1 tsp. olive oil
3 large red onions, thinly sliced
1 T. maple syrup or light brown sugar
1 T. balsamic vinegar
2 tsp. dried basil
2 C. marinara sauce
1 (10") unbaked pizza crust

4 C. shredded spinach
1/2 C. fresh chopped basil
1/2 C. crumbled feta cheese
1/2 tsp. dried oregano
1/4 tsp. pepper

Preheat oven to 375°. In a large skillet over medium heat, heat olive oil. Stir in sliced onions and sauté for about 10 minutes, or until onions are golden brown. Add maple syrup, vinegar and dried basil. Mix well, remove from heat and set aside. Spread marinara sauce evenly over unbaked pizza crust to within 1/2" of the edge. Arrange shredded spinach over sauce and top with sautéed onions. Sprinkle fresh basil, crumbled feta cheese, dried oregano and pepper evenly over onions. Bake in oven for 30 to 35 minutes, or until crust is crisp. Remove from oven and cut into slices before serving.

Russians serve pizza covered in mockba, a mixture of sardines, tuna, mackerel, salmon and onions.

Four Cheese Pizza

Makes 1 (12") pizza

1 (10 oz.) tube
  refrigerated pizza
  crust dough
1/3 C. grated Parmesan
  cheese
1 T. dried basil
1 C. shredded provolone
  cheese

1 C. shredded Cheddar
  cheese
1 C. shredded Monterey
  Jack cheese
1/2 C. pizza sauce

Preheat oven to 425°. Grease a 12" pizza pan. Roll out pizza crust dough and press firmly into bottom and up sides of prepared pizza pan. Bake in oven for 7 to 9 minutes, or until lightly browned. Remove partially baked crust from oven and sprinkle grated Parmesan cheese and dried basil over crust. Cover with shredded provolone cheese, shredded Cheddar cheese and shredded Monterey Jack cheese. Top pizza with spoonfuls of pizza sauce, spreading evenly. Bake in oven for 12 to 18 minutes, or until pizza crust is golden brown. Remove from oven and cut into slices before serving.

No-Sauce Veggie Pizza Pie

Makes 1 (12") pizza

1 (10 oz.) tube
   refrigerated pizza
   crust dough
Fresh baby spinach
   leaves

1/4 lb. sliced mushrooms
1/4 onion, chopped
2 C. shredded
   mozzarella cheese
1 tsp. dried oregano

Preheat oven to 425°. Lightly grease a 12" pizza pan. Roll out pizza crust dough and press firmly into bottom and up sides of prepared pizza pan. Spread baby spinach leaves evenly over crust to within 1/2" of the edge. Layer sliced mushrooms over spinach leaves and spread chopped onions over mushrooms. Cover evenly with shredded mozzarella cheese and dried oregano. Bake in oven for 15 to 18 minutes, or until cheese is bubbly and crust is golden brown. Remove from oven and cut into slices before serving.

Some popular pizza toppings in India are pickled ginger, minced mutton and tofu.

Philly Cheese Steak Pizza

Makes 1 (12") pizza

1 lb. ground beef
1 medium onion,
   thinly sliced
1 small green pepper,
   thinly sliced
1/2 tsp. salt

1/2 tsp. pepper
1 (12") pre-baked
   pizza crust
2 C. shredded
   mozzarella cheese

Preheat oven to 400°. In a large skillet over medium high heat, combine ground beef, sliced onion and sliced green pepper. Cook 5 to 7 minutes, until beef is cooked throughout and vegetables are softened. Drain off fat and add salt and pepper, mixing well. Place pre-baked pizza crust on a greased 12" pizza pan. Spread ground beef mixture evenly over crust and sprinkle with shredded mozzarella cheese. Bake in oven for 8 to 10 minutes, or until cheese is melted. Remove from oven and cut into slices before serving.

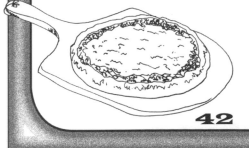

Tropical Shrimp Pizza

Makes 1 (12") pizza

1 (12") pre-baked
  pizza crust
1/4 C. pizza sauce
2 T. drained pineapple
  chunks
1/2 small banana, sliced

1/4 C. peeled, de-veined
  and cooked shrimp
1 C. shredded mozzarella
  cheese
1 T. shredded coconut

Preheat oven to 425°. Place pre-baked pizza crust on a lightly greased 12" pizza pan. Spread pizza sauce evenly over prepared crust. Layer pineapple chunks, banana slices, cooked shrimp and shredded mozzarella cheese over sauce on crust. Top with shredded coconut. Bake in oven 10 to 15 minutes, or until cheese is melted and slightly brown. Remove from oven and cut into slices before serving. Serve hot.

The first pizza was probably made about 1,000 years ago in Naples, Italy, when it became popular to cover flat baked dough with herbs and spices.

Alfredo Crab Pizza

Makes 1 (12") pizza

1 (12") pre-baked
   pizza crust
1 C. prepared alfredo
   sauce
2 C. imitation or
   cooked, shredded
   crabmeat
1 C. shredded Cheddar
   cheese

1 C. shredded
   mozzarella cheese
1 T. Italian seasoning
2 green onions, sliced
   thin
1 C. sliced mushrooms
8 slices bacon, cooked
   and crumbled

Preheat oven to 425°. Place pre-baked pizza crust on a lightly greased 12" pizza pan. Spread prepared alfredo sauce evenly over crust. Place imitation or cooked crabmeat over the sauce and sprinkle with shredded Cheddar cheese and shredded mozzarella cheese. In a small bowl, toss together Italian seasoning, sliced green onions, sliced mushrooms and cooked bacon. Spread mixture over cheese on crust. Bake in oven for 20 to 25 minutes, until cheese is melted. Remove from oven and cut into slices before serving.

Spaghetti Pizza Pie

Makes 1 (9") Pie

1 lb. ground beef
1/2 C. dry breadcrumbs
1/4 C. finely chopped
   onions
1 tsp. salt
1/2 tsp. pepper
2/3 C. evaporated milk
1 egg, beaten
1/4 C. grated Parmesan
   cheese

2 T. butter or margarine
4 oz. spaghetti noodles,
   cooked and drained
1 C. pizza sauce
1 C. shredded mozzarella
   cheese
1 green bell pepper,
   sliced into rings

Preheat oven to 350°. In a large bowl, combine ground beef, dry breadcrumbs, chopped onions, salt, pepper and evaporated milk. Mix well and press ground beef mixture firmly into the bottom and up sides of a 9" pie plate. Bake in oven for 35 to 40 minutes. Remove from oven and drain drippings off of meat layer. In a large bowl, toss together beaten egg, grated Parmesan cheese, butter and cooked spaghetti noodles. Spread the spaghetti mixture over the baked ground beef mixture in pie pan. Top with pizza sauce. Sprinkle shredded mozzarella cheese over sauce and top with green pepper rings. Return to oven for an additional 10 minutes. Remove from oven and let stand 5 minutes before cutting into slices.

Gourmet Chicken Pizza

Makes 1 (12") pizza

1 (10 oz.) can
    refrigerated pizza
    crust dough
2 skinless, boneless
    chicken breast halves
1/2 C. ranch dressing
1 C. shredded
    mozzarella cheese

1 C. chopped tomatoes
1/4 C. chopped green
    onions
1 C. shredded Cheddar
    cheese

Preheat oven to 425°. Lightly grease a 12" pizza pan. Roll out pizza crust dough and press evenly on the bottom and up sides of prepared pan. Bake in oven for 7 minutes, or until crust is golden brown. Remove from oven and set aside. In a large skillet over medium high heat, sauté chicken breast halves until juices run clear and chicken is no longer pink. Remove chicken from skillet and chop into small pieces. Spread ranch dressing evenly over warm pizza crust. Sprinkle shredded mozzarella cheese over crust and layer with chopped tomatoes, chopped green onions and cooked chicken. Sprinkle shredded Cheddar cheese over chicken. Bake in oven for 20 to 25 minutes, or until cheese is melted. Remove from oven and cut into slices before serving.

Pineapple Teriyaki Chicken Pizza

Makes 1 (16") pizza

1 (15 oz.) can pineapple
   chunks
2 skinless boneless
   chicken breast
   halves, cut into
   small pieces
1 tsp. minced garlic
2 (10 oz.) cans
   refrigerated pizza
   crust dough

1 C. teriyaki sauce
1 small sweet onion,
   thinly sliced
1 C. shredded Cheddar
   cheese
1 C. crumbled feta cheese

Drain pineapple, reserving the juice. In a small baking dish, combine reserved pineapple juice, chicken pieces and minced garlic. Cover and place in refrigerator for 1 hour. Preheat oven to 400°. Remove chicken pieces from pineapple juice. In a large skillet over high heat, sauté chicken until slightly browned and cooked throughout. Roll out refrigerated dough to fit a 16" pizza pan. Place dough on pan and bake in oven for 7 minutes. Remove crust from oven and brush lightly with teriyaki sauce. Place a layer of sliced onion over teriyaki sauce and top with shredded Cheddar cheese. Arrange chicken pieces, pineapple chunks and crumbled feta cheese over the pizza. Return to oven for an additional 15 minutes, or until cheese is melted and lightly browned. Remove from oven and cut into slices before serving.

Upside Down Pizza

Makes 8 servings

1 lb. ground beef
1 C. chopped onions
1 (14 oz.) jar spaghetti
  sauce
2 C. shredded
  mozzarella cheese

1 C. milk
2 eggs
1 tsp. vegetable oil
1 C. flour
1/2 tsp. salt

Preheat oven to 400°. In a large skillet over medium heat, cook ground beef and onions until beef is cooked throughout and onions are softened. Drain off fat and add sauce. Continue to cook until mixture is heated throughout. Pour mixture into a 9x13" baking dish. Sprinkle shredded mozzarella cheese over ingredients in baking dish. In a large bowl, combine milk, eggs, vegetable oil, flour and salt, mixing until well combined. Pour mixture over mozzarella cheese. Bake in oven for 30 minutes, or until golden brown. Remove from oven and cut into slices before serving.

Pepperoni Stuffed-Crust Pizza

Makes 8 servings

1 (10 oz.) can refrigerated pizza crust dough
7 pieces string cheese

1/2 C. pizza sauce
20 slices pepperoni
1 C. shredded mozzarella cheese

Preheat oven to 425°. Lightly grease a 9x13" baking dish. Press refrigerated pizza crust dough into bottom and 1" up sides of baking dish. Arrange string cheese in a single layer around the edge of the pizza dough. Fold the dough from the sides down over the pieces of string cheese. Press the edges tightly to seal the cheese inside. Spread pizza sauce evenly over pizza dough. Top with pepperoni slices and shredded mozzarella cheese. Bake in oven for 15 to 18 minutes, or until cheese melts and crust is golden brown. Remove from oven and cut into slices before serving.

Pizza was originally an Italian peasant food, designed to be eaten without utensils and as a great way to use leftovers.

Mexican Pizza

Makes 1 (12") pizza

**1 (12") pre-baked
  pizza crust**
1/2 lb. ground beef
**1 (15 1/2 oz.) can
  chili beans**
**1 (8 oz.) can corn,
  drained**

**2 T. chopped green
  chilies**
**1 C. shredded
  Cheddar cheese**
3 green onions, chopped
6 olives, sliced
2 tomatoes, chopped

Preheat oven to 425°. Place pre-baked pizza crust on a 12" pizza pan. In a medium skillet over medium heat, brown ground beef until cooked throughout and drain off fat. Add chili beans, drained corn and chopped green chilies to skillet and mix well. Spread ground beef mixture evenly over pizza crust. Top with shredded Cheddar cheese, chopped green onions, sliced olives and chopped tomatoes. Bake in oven for 10 to 12 minutes, or until cheese melts. Remove from oven and cut into slices before serving.

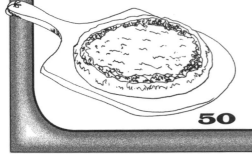

BBQ Chicken Pizza

Makes 1 (12") pizza

1 (12") pre-baked pizza
   crust
3 boneless chicken
   breast halves, cooked
   and cubed
1 C. barbecue sauce
1 T. honey
1 tsp. molasses

1/3 C. brown sugar
1/4 C. fresh chopped
   cilantro
1 C. shredded smoked
   Gouda cheese
1 C. thinly sliced red
   onions

Preheat oven to 425°. Place pre-baked pizza crust on a 12" pizza pan. In a large saucepan over medium heat, combine cooked chicken, barbecue sauce, honey, molasses, brown sugar and cilantro. Bring mixture to a boil. Remove from heat and spread mixture evenly over pizza crust. Top with shredded Gouda cheese and sliced red onions. Bake in oven for 15 to 20 minutes, or until cheese is melted. Remove from oven and cut into slices before serving.

The world's first pizzeria, named Port'Alba, first opened in 1830.

51

Meatball Pizza

Makes 1 (12") pizza

1 (12") pre-baked pizza
   crust
1 (14 oz.) jar pizza
   sauce, divided
1 1/2 C. shredded
   Cheddar cheese,
   divided

1 1/2 to 2 C. small
   frozen or homemade
   meatballs
1/4 tsp. dried Italian
   seasoning

Preheat oven to 400°. Place pre-baked pizza crust on a 12" pizza pan. Spread 1 cup pizza sauce evenly over the crust and sprinkle 1 cup shredded Cheddar cheese over the sauce. In a small bowl, combine meatballs with remaining pizza sauce. Spoon meatballs and sauce over the crust. Top with remaining 1/2 cup shredded Cheddar cheese and Italian seasoning. Bake in oven 20 minutes, or until cheese is melted. Remove from oven and cut into slices before serving.

The popularity of pizza exploded throughout the United States when World War II servicemen returning from Italy raved about the "great Italian dish" and began opening pizzerias.

Potato Bacon Pizza

Makes 1 (12") pizza

3 large potatoes,
    peeled and cubed
1 (10 oz.) can
    refrigerated pizza
    crust dough
1/4 C. milk
1 T. garlic powder
1/2 tsp. salt
1 lb. bacon, chopped

1 large onion, chopped
1/2 C. chopped
    red peppers
1 1/2 C. shredded
    mozzarella cheese
1 1/2 C. shredded
    Cheddar cheese
Sour cream, optional

Preheat oven to 350°. In a medium pot over medium high heat, place cubed potatoes. Fill pot with water and bring to a boil. Continue to boil until potatoes are tender. Press refrigerated pizza crust into bottom and up sides of a 12" pizza pan. Using a fork, poke holes in the bottom of the crust and bake in oven for 15 minutes. Remove from oven and set crust aside. Increase oven temperature to 375°. In a large mixing bowl, place the drained potatoes. Add milk, garlic powder and salt. Mix at medium speed, until potatoes are smooth. Spread potato mixture evenly over the pizza crust. In a large skillet over medium heat, cook bacon until partially crisp. Add chopped onion and chopped red peppers. Continue to heat until bacon is crisp and vegetables are tender. Drain off fat and sprinkle bacon mixture over mashed potatoes on pizza. Sprinkle shredded mozzarella cheese and shredded Cheddar cheese over bacon mixture. Bake in oven for 20 minutes. Remove from oven and cut into slices before serving. If desired, serve with sour cream on the side.

Grilled Meat 'n Veggie Pizza

Makes 2 (8") pizzas

1 lb. ground beef	2 C. shredded
3/4 C. spaghetti sauce	mozzarella cheese
1/2 C. spicy steak sauce	1/4 C. chopped tomatoes
1 lb. frozen bread or	1/4 C. sliced green onions
pizza dough, thawed	1/4 C. sliced ripe olives
2 T. olive oil	

In a large skillet over medium high heat, brown ground beef until cooked throughout. Drain skillet of fat and stir in spaghetti sauce and spicy steak sauce. Cook until mixture is thoroughly heated. Reduce heat and keep mixture warm over stovetop. Shape thawed dough into two 8" rounds. Using a pastry brush, cover each round lightly with olive oil. Place pizzas, oiled side down, onto a preheated grill. Grill until dough is firm and lightly browned, approximately 5 to 7 minutes. Brush the top side of each pizza with remaining olive oil and flip the crusts over. Divide the ground beef mixture, shredded mozzarella cheese, chopped tomatoes, sliced green onions and sliced olives evenly over the two pizza crusts. Cover grill and let pizzas cook for 5 to 7 minutes, until crust is golden brown and cheese has melted. Carefully remove pizzas from grill and cut into slices before serving.

Grilled Onion Ranch Pizza

Makes 1 (12") pizza

1 (12") pre-baked
    pizza crust
1/2 C. ranch dressing
1 C. crumbled feta cheese

1/2 C. chopped red onions
1/4 C. olives
1 C. chopped cucumbers,
    optional

Preheat grill to medium heat. Cover a large baking sheet with aluminum foil. Place the pre-baked pizza crust on the covered baking sheet and spread ranch dressing in an even layer over pizza crust. Crumble feta cheese over crust and top pizza with chopped red onions and chopped olives. Carefully slide pizza, with foil underneath, onto the hot grill. Cover grill and cook pizza for 10 to 15 minutes, or until crust is lightly browned. Carefully remove pizza from grill and cut into slices. If desired, top with chopped cucumbers before serving.

In 1905, Gennaro Lombardi opened the first licensed American pizzeria, Lombardi's Pizzeria Napoletana, at 53 1/2 Spring Street in New York City.

Hawaiian BBQ Chicken Pizza

Makes 1 (12") pizza

1 (12") pre-baked
  pizza crust
Olive oil
1 (1/2 lb.) chicken breast
1 3/4 C. barbecue sauce,
  divided
2 C. shredded mozzarella
  cheese, divided

1 small red onion,
  thinly sliced
3 slices bacon, cooked
  and crumbled
1 (10 oz.) can pineapple
  tidbits, drained
Parsley for garnish

Preheat oven to 450°. Place pre-baked pizza crust on a lightly greased 12" pizza pan. Using a pastry brush, brush the crust with olive oil. In a large skillet over medium heat, place chicken breast. Cook chicken breast until heated throughout and no longer pink. Remove chicken from skillet and shred chicken meat into small pieces. Return shredded chicken to skillet and add 1 cup barbecue sauce. Simmer mixture for 5 to 10 minutes. Spread remaining 3/4 cup barbecue sauce over pizza crust. Sprinkle 1 cup shredded mozzarella cheese evenly over the sauce. Layer shredded chicken mixture, red onion slices, crumbled bacon, drained pineapple tidbits and remaining 1 cup mozzarella cheese evenly over pizza. Reduce oven temperature to 425°. Bake in oven for 12 minutes. For a crisper crust, remove pizza from pan and place pizza directly on oven rack for an additional 3 minutes. Remove pizza from oven and garnish with fresh chopped parsley. Let cool 5 minutes before cutting into slices and serving.

Buffalo
Chicken Pizza

Makes 1 (16") pizza

1 (16") pre-baked
   pizza crust
1 (16 oz.) bottle blue
   cheese dressing
3 chicken breast halves,
   cooked and cubed

2 T. butter, melted
1 (2 oz.) bottle hot sauce
1 C. shredded
   mozzarella cheese

    Preheat oven to 425°. Place pre-baked pizza crust on a lightly greased 16" pizza pan or large baking sheet. Spread blue cheese dressing evenly over the pizza crust. In a large bowl, combine cooked cubed chicken, melted butter and hot sauce, tossing until evenly coated. Spread chicken mixture evenly over blue cheese layer on pizza. Top with shredded mozzarella cheese. Bake in oven 5 to 10 minutes, or until crust is golden brown and cheese melted. Let stand 3 minutes before cutting into slices and serving.

It is believed the deep-dish pizza was invented in Chicago by pizza entrepreneur, Ike Sewell, in his downtown Chicago restaurant, Pizzeria Uno.

Vegetables Florentine Pizza

Make 1 (12") pizza

1 (12") pre-baked
   pizza crust
Olive oil
3/4 C. pizza sauce
2 C. shredded mozzarella
   cheese, divided
5 cloves garlic, minced
1 small onion,
   thinly sliced
1 medium green pepper,
   thinly sliced

1/2 medium red pepper,
   thinly sliced
1 T. Italian dressing
2 C. fresh chopped spinach
3 T. fresh chopped cilantro
2 Roma tomatoes,
   peeled and sliced
1/2 C. grated Parmesan
   cheese

Preheat oven to 450°. Place pre-baked pizza crust on a lightly greased 12" pizza pan. Using a pastry brush, brush olive oil over crust. Spread pizza sauce evenly over the crust and sprinkle 1 cup shredded mozzarella cheese evenly over sauce and set aside. In a medium skillet over medium heat, combine minced garlic, sliced onion, sliced green pepper and sliced red pepper. Add a little Italian dressing and sauté vegetables until tender. Spread sautéed mixture over mozzarella cheese on crust. In same skillet over medium heat, place fresh chopped spinach and fresh chopped cilantro. Sauté vegetables until spinach is slightly limp. Spread spinach mixture over onion mixture on pizza. Arrange sliced tomatoes over pizza and sprinkle grated Parmesan and remaining 1 cup shredded mozzarella over tomatoes. Reduce oven temperature to 425°. Bake in oven for 12 minutes. For a crisper crust, remove pizza from pan and place pizza directly on oven rack for an additional 3 minutes. Remove pizza from oven and let cool 5 minutes before cutting into slices and serving.

Easy Three Cheese Pepperoni Pizza

Makes 1 (12") pizza

**1 (12") pre-baked
pizza crust**
Olive oil
1 C. pizza sauce
**1/2 C. shredded
Cheddar cheese**

**1/2 C. shredded
mozzarella cheese**
**1/4 C. crumbled
feta cheese**
**1 (3 1/2 oz.) pkg.
pepperoni slices**

Preheat oven to 450°. Place pre-baked pizza crust directly on oven rack for 2 to 3 minutes, remove crust from oven and brush with a thin layer of olive oil. Spread pizza sauce evenly over crust. Layer shredded Cheddar cheese, shredded mozzarella cheese and crumbled feta cheese evenly over the sauce. Arrange pepperoni slices over cheese on pizza. Reduce oven temperature to 425°. Bake pizza directly on oven rack and bake for 8 to 10 minutes, or until cheese melts. Remove pizza from oven and let cool 5 minutes before cutting into slices and serving.

According to a recent poll of pizza delivery folks, it was reported that women are better tippers than men!

Chicken Enchilada Pizza

Makes 1 (12") pizza

1 (12") pre-baked
    pizza crust
Olive oil
2/3 C. enchilada sauce
1/3 C. sour cream
2 C. shredded Colby
    Jack cheese, divided
1 (14 1/2 oz.) can diced
    tomatoes with green
    chilies, drained

1/2 C. finely chopped
    onions
1 1/2 C. cooked, diced
    chicken
1 C. crushed corn chips

Preheat oven to 450°. Place pre-baked pizza crust on a lightly greased 12" pizza pan. Using a pastry brush, brush olive oil over crust. In a medium bowl, combine enchilada sauce and sour cream. Mix well and spread over pizza crust. Sprinkle 1/2 cup shredded cheese over sauce. Top pizza with drained tomatoes, chopped onions and cooked diced chicken. Sprinkle 1 cup shredded cheese over chicken. In a small bowl, combine crushed corn chips and remaining 1/2 cup shredded cheese. Spread mixture over ingredients on pizza. Reduce oven temperature to 425°. Bake in oven for 12 minutes. For a crisper crust, remove pizza from pan and place pizza directly on oven rack for an additional 3 minutes. Remove pizza from oven and let cool 5 minutes before cutting into slices and serving.

Simple Pesto Pizza Pie

Makes 1 (12") pizza

**1 (12") pre-baked
  pizza crust
1/2 C. prepared pesto
  basil sauce
2 C. cooked chicken
  breast strips**

**1 (6 oz.) jar artichoke
  hearts, drained
1/2 C. shredded fontina
  cheese**

Preheat oven to 450°. Place pizza crust on a lightly greased 12" pizza pan. Spread pesto sauce evenly over the crust. Arrange cooked chicken breast strips and artichoke hearts evenly over the sauce. Top with shredded fontina cheese. Bake in oven for 8 to 10 minutes, or until cheese melts and crust is lightly browned. Remove pizza from oven and let cool 5 minutes before cutting into slices and serving.

In America, anchovies continuously rank last on the list of favorite pizza toppings.

Basic Grilled Pizza

Makes 1 (12") pizza

1 (12") unbaked
   pizza crust
1 C. pizza sauce
2 C. shredded
   mozzarella cheese

1/2 C. chopped
   green peppers
1/2 C. fresh sliced
   mushrooms

Preheat grill to high heat and lightly oil grate. Place unbaked pizza crust on grill for 5 minutes and flip over. Spread tomato sauce evenly over crust and top with shredded mozzarella cheese. Arrange chopped green peppers and sliced mushrooms evenly over pizza. Cover grill and cook for 5 to 10 minutes, or until cheese is bubbly. Carefully remove pizza from grill, cut into slices and serve.

According to the National Restaurant Association, Italian foods ranks as the most popular ethnic food served in America.

Pizza
for
One

Pizzas with Goat Cheese & Red Peppers

Makes 8 individual pizzas

4 pita bread rounds
1 (11 oz.) log goat
  cheese, crumbled
1 (7 oz.) jar roasted
  red peppers, drained
  and chopped

1 C. chopped sun-dried
  tomatoes
1 C. fresh chopped basil
1/2 C. balsamic vinegar

Preheat oven to 400°. Make 2 rounds from each of the four pita breads by cutting the outer edge and carefully pulling the halves apart. Place the pita bread halves on large baking sheets. Sprinkle pita rounds with goat cheese, roasted red peppers and sun-dried tomatoes. Bake each pizza in oven for 16 minutes, or until the crust is crisp. Remove from oven and sprinkle with basil and drizzle with balsamic vinegar. Cut into slices and serve pizzas warm.

Hearty Chili Pizzas

Makes 6 individual pizzas

1 lb. ground beef
1 onion, chopped
1 (15 1/2 oz.) can
   chili with beans
1 (14 1/2 oz.) can diced
   tomatoes, drained

6 pita bread rounds
3 C. shredded
   mozzarella cheese

Preheat oven to 400°. In a large skillet over medium heat, brown the ground beef and onion. Drain the mixture of fat and stir in chili and diced tomatoes. Mix well. On a large baking sheet, place the pita bread rounds. Spread the beef mixture evenly over each pita bread and sprinkle with mozzarella cheese. Bake in oven for 10 to 12 minutes or until the mozzarella cheese is melted and the pitas are crisp. Cut into slices and serve pizzas warm.

In America, 62% of pizza customers prefer meat toppings, while 38% choose vegetarian toppings.

Pizza Pot Pies

Makes 4 individual pizzas

1 lb. Italian sausage,
   cut into 1" rounds
2 C. pizza sauce
1 C. shredded ricotta
   cheese
1/4 C. grated
   Parmesan cheese
1 T. Italian seasoning

1 tsp. garlic salt
1 egg, beaten
2 C. shredded
   mozzarella cheese,
   divided
1 tube refrigerated
   pizza crust dough

Preheat oven to 375°. In a medium skillet over medium high heat, place sausage pieces and heat for about 7 minutes, until browned and cooked throughout. Drain off fat and add pizza sauce. Divide mixture evenly into four oven-safe bowls or large ramekins. In a medium bowl, combine shredded ricotta cheese, grated Parmesan cheese, Italian seasoning, garlic salt and beaten egg. Stir until well combined and place 1/4 of the cheese mixture over each bowl. Sprinkle 1/2 cup shredded mozzarella cheese over each bowl. Unroll pizza crust dough and cut into four even squares. Place one dough square over ingredients in each bowl and tuck down edges inside of bowl. Using a fork, prick holes over crust and place bowls on a baking sheet. Bake in oven for about 30 minutes, or until topping is lightly browned. Remove from oven and let sit for 10 minutes before serving.

Pepperoni Mushroom Calzones

Makes 2 large calzones

1 (1/4 oz.) pkg. active cheese
    dry yeast
1 C. warm water
1 T. plus 1 tsp. olive
    oil, divided
1 tsp. sugar
1 tsp. salt
2 1/2 C. flour, divided

1/2 C. grated ricotta

1 1/2 C. shredded
    Cheddar cheese
1/2 C. diced pepperoni
1/2 C. sliced fresh
    mushrooms
1 T. dried basil
1 egg, beate

In a small bowl, dissolve yeast in warm water. Add 1 tablespoon olive oil, sugar and salt. Mix in 1 cup flour, stirring until smooth. Gradually stir in remaining 1 1/2 cups flour, until dough is workable. On a lightly floured surface, knead dough for 5 minutes or until elastic in consistency. Place remaining 1 teaspoon olive oil in a large bowl and set dough over oil. Flip dough, cover with a kitchen towel and let rise for 40 minutes, or until dough has doubled in size. In a separate large bowl, combine ricotta cheese, Cheddar cheese, diced pepperoni, sliced mushrooms and basil. Mix well and place in refrigerator. Preheat oven to 375°. Punch down dough and divide into 2 equal parts. On a lightly floured surface, roll each portion into a thin circle. Divide filling mixture evenly over the two circles. Fold circles over and press edges with a fork to seal. Place calzones on a lightly greased baking sheet. Brush tops with beaten egg. Bake in oven for 30 minutes.

Spinach Artichoke Calzones

Makes 6 individual calzones

1 (14 oz.) can artichoke
hearts, drained and
chopped
1 clove garlic, minced
1/4 tsp. salt
1/4 tsp. pepper
1 C. fresh chopped
spinach

1 C. shredded Swiss
cheese
1/2 C. cooked, chopped
ham
1 (13.8 oz.) tube
refrigerated pizza
crust dough

Preheat oven to 425°. Grease a large baking sheet. In a large bowl, combine the chopped artichoke hearts, minced garlic, salt and pepper, mixing well. Add chopped spinach, shredded Swiss cheese and cooked ham. Mix gently and spread out pizza crust dough on the prepared baking sheet. Cut dough into six 5" squares. Divide spinach mixture equally among the squares and fold over diagonally to make triangles. Seal edges by pinching together. Spray calzones with cooking spray. Bake in oven for 12 to 15 minutes, or until golden brown. Serve immediately.

Grilled Pizza Wraps

Makes 8 individual wraps

2 T. margarine, softened	1 C. shredded Cheddar and Monterey Jack cheese blend
8 (10") tortillas	
1/2 C. pizza sauce	1/4 C. sliced pepperoni

Spread softened margarine over one side of each tortilla. In a large skillet over medium heat, place one tortilla at a time, buttered side down. Spread 1 tablespoon pizza sauce evenly over half of the tortilla. Sprinkle 1/2 cup cheese over sauce. Top with sliced pepperoni. Fold tortilla in half over the filling. Cook, carefully turning once, until tortilla is golden brown. Repeat with remaining tortillas.

Women are twice as likely as men to order vegetables to top their pizza.

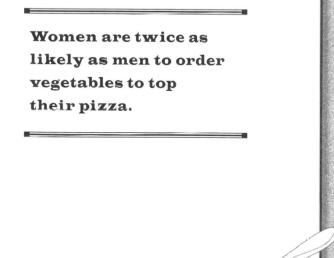

Red Pepper Pizza Grilled Sandwiches

Makes 2 sandwiches

4 slices white bread	2 T. chopped red peppers
2 T. pizza sauce	2 T. chopped red onions
4 slices mozzarella cheese	4 tsp. margarine, softened

Spread pizza sauce evenly over 2 slices of bread. Over sauce on each slice of bread, place 1 mozzarella slice, 1 tablespoon chopped red peppers and 1 tablespoon chopped red onions. Top with another mozzarella slice and remaining bread slices. Spread softened margarine on both sides of each sandwich. In a large skillet over medium heat, cook sandwiches for 3 minutes on each side, or until lightly browned.

In France, a popular pizza topping is Flambée, a combination of bacon, onions and fresh cream.

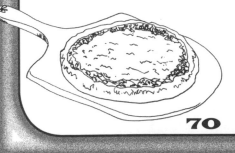

Mexican Chicken Pizzas

Makes 4 individual pizzas

8 (10") flour tortillas
2 C. shredded Monterey
   Jack cheese, divided
1 C. salsa, any kind
2 C. cooked, chopped
   chicken
2 jalapenos, diced
1/2 C. sliced black olives

2 tomatoes, thinly sliced
1 small onion, thinly
   sliced
1 (8 oz.) container
   sour cream, optional
Guacamole, optional
Fresh chopped cilantro,
   optional

Preheat oven to 400°. On a large baking sheet, place 4 tortillas. Spread 1/4 cup shredded Monterey Jack cheese over each tortilla and cover with remaining 4 tortillas. Spread the salsa, cooked chicken, jalapenos, olives, tomatoes and onions evenly over each tortilla pizza. Divide the remaining 1 cup cheese evenly over each pizza. Bake in oven for 15 to 20 minutes, or until cheese begins to bubble. Remove from oven and, if desired, top with sour cream, guacamole and cilantro.

Mini Bagel Bites

Make 12 individual bites

**6 mini bagels, split
and toasted
1/4 C. pizza sauce**

**3/4 C. shredded
cheese, any kind**

Preheat oven to broil. On a large baking sheet, place split bagel halves, cut side up. Spread pizza sauce evenly over each bagel half and sprinkle with shredded cheese. Place bagels under broiler for 2 to 3 minutes, or until cheese is melted. Serve warm.

Australians often choose shrimp, pineapple and barbecued toppings for their pizzas.

Cheeseburger Pizzas

Makes 8 individual pizzas

1/2 lb. ground beef
1/2 C. diced pepperoni
1 1/4 C. pizza sauce
1 C. crumbled feta cheese
1/2 tsp. Worcestershire
  sauce
1/2 tsp. hot pepper
  sauce

Salt and pepper, to taste
1 (10 oz.) can
  refrigerated biscuit
  dough
1 egg yolk
1 C. shredded
  mozzarella cheese

Preheat oven to 375°. In a large skillet over medium heat, brown ground beef and drain. Stir in diced pepperoni, pizza sauce and crumbled feta cheese. Add Worcestershire sauce, hot pepper sauce, salt and pepper. Cook for 1 minute, stirring constantly. Grease a large baking sheet. Separate biscuits and place 3" apart on the prepared baking sheet. Press each biscuit with the bottom of a glass, forming a 1/2" ridge around the outside edge of each biscuit. In a small bowl, beat egg yolk with 1/4 teaspoon water. Brush egg mixture over sides and edges of biscuits. Spoon 1/4 cup beef mixture into each biscuit. Top with sprinkled mozzarella cheese. Bake in oven for 15 to 20 minutes, or until golden brown and cheese bubbles. Let cool for 2 minutes before serving.

Easy Pita Pizzas

Makes 6 individual pizzas

6 pita bread rounds
1 (6 1/2 oz.) can
   tomato sauce
1 (4 oz.) can sliced
   black olives, drained
1 (1 oz.) can diced
   pimento peppers,
   drained
2 small tomatoes,
   thinly sliced

1/4 C. shredded
   mozzarella cheese
1/4 C. crumbled blue
   cheese
Pinch of dried basil
Pinch of dried oregano
Pinch of dried
   coriander seed

Preheat oven to 425°. On a large baking sheet, place the pita bread rounds and warm in oven for 1 minute, or until bread is softened. Spread tomato sauce evenly over pita rounds, pressing down firmly with the back of a spoon to flatten bread. Sprinkle sliced black olives, pimento peppers, sliced tomatoes, shredded mozzarella cheese, crumbled blue cheese, basil, oregano and coriander on each pita round. Bake in oven for 8 minutes, or until pita breads are crisp. Cut into slices and serve pizzas warm.

Hawaiian
Pita Pizza

Makes 1 individual pizza

1 (4") pita bread
   round
1/4 C. pizza sauce
4 slices cooked ham

1/4 C. drained pineapple
   chunks
1/2 C. shredded
   Monterey Jack cheese

Preheat oven to 400°. On a small baking sheet, place the pita bread round. Spread pizza sauce evenly over top of the pita round. Place sliced ham and pineapple chunks evenly over sauce. Sprinkle with shredded Monterey Jack cheese. Bake in oven for 12 to 15 minutes, or until cheese is melted and golden brown. Serve warm.

**In Costa Rica, coconut is a
popular topping for pizza.**

Mini Pizza Rounds

Makes 4 individual pizzas

1 lb. ground beef	1/2 tsp. salt
1/2 C. chopped onion	1/4 tsp. pepper
1 (8 oz.) can tomato	1 C. cubed American
soup	cheese
1 tsp. dried oregano	8 hamburger buns
Dash of garlic salt	

Preheat oven to 325°. In a large skillet over medium heat, brown ground beef and chopped onion, heating until ground beef is cooked throughout. Drain off fat and stir in tomato soup, dried oregano, garlic salt, salt, pepper and cubed American cheese. Continue to heat until cheese is completely melted, stirring occasionally. On a large baking sheet, place hamburger buns. Top each hamburger bun with a generous amount of the ground beef mixture. Bake in oven for 8 minutes. Serve pizzas warm.

In Pakistan, curry-flavored pizza is popular.

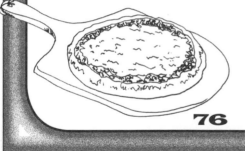

76

Apple & Feta Pan Pizzas

Makes 8 individual pizzas

1 (6 1/2 oz.) pkg.
   pizza crust mix
1/2 C. hot water
5 T. olive oil
1 C. crumbled feta
   cheese
1 red onion, thinly
   sliced

1 T. plus 1 tsp. fresh
   chopped thyme
1/2 T. butter
4 apples, cored and
   chopped
Pepper, to taste

Preheat oven to 300˚. In a medium bowl, combine pizza crust mix and hot water. Stir well until thoroughly blended. Let stand in a warm place for 5 minutes. Divide dough into 8 even sections. On a lightly floured surface, knead each section and form into circles. In a large skillet over medium heat, heat olive oil. Carefully set dough rounds in hot oil and fry, turning once, until lightly browned on both sides. Remove, drain slightly and place fried dough circles on a large baking sheet. In a small bowl, combine crumbled feta, sliced red onion and 1 tablespoon chopped thyme. Mix lightly and sprinkle mixture evenly over each round. Bake in oven for 10 to 12 minutes, or until cheese is lightly browned. Meanwhile, in the same large skillet, combine butter and remaining 1 teaspoon chopped thyme. Add chopped apples and sauté until apples are softened and golden brown. Remove pizzas from oven and top with cooked apple mixture. Sprinkle with pepper to taste and serve pizzas immediately.

Italian Sausage & Pineapple Pizzas

Makes 8 individual pizzas

1/2 lb. ground Italian sausage	4 English muffins, halved
1/2 tsp. garlic salt	1 (6 oz.) can tomato paste
1/4 tsp. dried oregano	1 (8 oz.) pkg. shredded mozzarella cheese
1 C. drained pineapple chunks	

Preheat oven to 350°. In a large deep skillet over medium heat, brown Italian sausage until cooked throughout. Remove from heat and drain off fat. Add garlic salt, dried oregano and crushed pineapple, mixing until well combined. Grease a large baking sheet and arrange English muffin halves in a single layer. Spread an even amount of the tomato paste over each half. Divide the sausage and pineapple mixture evenly over each English muffin half and sprinkle each with shredded mozzarella cheese. Bake in oven for 10 to 15 minutes, or until cheese is melted and lightly browned. Serve pizzas warm.

Crusts
and
Sauces

Basic Pizza Crust

Makes 1 pizza crust

1 (1/4 oz.) pkg.
   active dry yeast
2/3 C. warm water,
   divided

2 to 2 1/4 C. flour
1/2 tsp. sugar
2 T. olive oil
1/2 tsp. salt

In a large mixing bowl, dissolve yeast in 1/3 cup warm water and let stand for 5 minutes. Add 2 cups flour, sugar, olive oil, salt and the remaining 1/3 cup warm water. Knead mixture by hand until smooth, adding additional flour as needed. Place dough in a large greased bowl and cover with a kitchen towel. Set aside in a warm place until dough doubles in size. Remove from bowl, punch down, and roll out dough to desired size. Press dough onto a greased pizza pan and cover with desired toppings. Bake as desired.

A Double Dutch pizza, which is covered with double cheese, double onions and double beef, is a favorite in the Netherlands.

Soft-on-the-Inside Pizza Crust

Makes 1 large or 2 small pizza crusts

2 1/4 tsp. active dry yeast	1 tsp. salt
1/2 tsp. brown sugar	2 T. olive oil
1 1/2 C. warm water	3 1/3 C. flour

Preheat oven to 425°. In a large mixing bowl, combine yeast, brown sugar and warm water. Mix lightly until yeast is completely dissolved. Let stand for 10 minutes. Stir salt and olive oil into the yeast mixture. Gradually mix in flour until a soft dough forms. Knead dough on a lightly floured flat surface until no longer sticky. Place dough in a well greased bowl, cover with a kitchen towel and let stand for approximately 1 hour, or until doubled in size. Remove dough from bowl and punch down. Form dough into a tight ball and let sit for 1 minute before rolling out flat. If desired, the dough can be baked immediately on a pizza stone. If using a pizza pan, spread dough over lightly greased pan and let rise for 15 to 20 minutes before topping with desired ingredients and baking. Bake in oven for 15 to 20 minutes.

Pizza Shop
Pizza Crust

Makes 1 pizza crust

1 1/4 tsp. active dry yeast	1 T. sugar
2 C. bread flour	1 T. dry milk powder
1 tsp. salt	1 T. margarine, softened
	1/3 C. warm water

Preheat oven to 375°. In a large mixing bowl, combine yeast, flour, salt, sugar, dry milk powder, softened margarine and warm water. Mix well and form dough into a ball. Place the dough on a lightly floured flat surface and knead by hand until smooth. Place dough into a large greased bowl and turn to lightly coat the surface of the dough with oil. Cover dough with a kitchen towel and set aside in a warm place for 2 hours. Remove dough from bowl and punch down. Roll out dough and place in greased pizza pan. Let dough rise until doubled in size before adding desired toppings and baking. Bake in oven for 20 minutes.

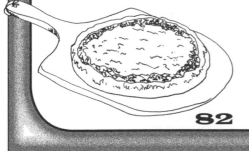

Sweet Whole Wheat Pizza Crust

Makes 1 pizza crust

1 (1/4 oz.) pkg.
   active dry yeast
1 C. warm water
1 C. whole wheat flour

1/4 C. wheat germ
1 tsp. salt
1 T. honey

Preheat oven to 350°. In a small mixing bowl, dissolve yeast in warm water. Let stand for about 10 minutes, until mixture is foamy. In a large mixing bowl, combine wheat flour, wheat germ and salt. Form a well in the center of the flour mixture and pour yeast mixture and honey into the well. Stir well, cover with a kitchen towel and set aside in a warm place for about 5 minutes. Once dough has risen, remove from bowl and roll out onto a floured 12" pizza pan. Using a fork, prick a few holes in the bottom of the crust. Top crust with desired toppings and bake in oven for 5 to 10 minutes, or until crust is crisp.

Pizza Hut is the largest pizza vendor in the world, with more than 12,500 restaurants in the United States and more than 90 other countries worldwide.

Bread Machine Garlic Pizza Crust

Makes 1 pizza crust

6 oz. warm water
2 T. olive oil
3 cloves garlic, minced
2 C. bread flour

1 tsp. sugar
1/2 tsp. salt
2 tsp. active dry yeast

Preheat oven to 400°. Combine ingredients in bread machine pan as recommended by the bread machine manufacturer. Select dough cycle and press Start. When dough cycle has ended, remove dough from machine and knead on a lightly floured flat surface. Form dough into a tight ball, place in a greased bowl and let stand for 15 minutes. Remove from bowl and stretch dough to fit a 14" pizza pan. Let dough stand for 20 minutes before topping with desired ingredients. Bake in oven for 10 to 20 minutes, or until crust is lightly browned.

Italian Pizza Crust

Makes 1 large pizza crust

1 C. warm water
3 T. olive oil
3 T. sugar
1 tsp. salt
2 1/2 C. bread flour

2 tsp. minced garlic
2 1/4 tsp. active dry yeast
1/2 tsp. dried oregano
1/2 tsp. dried basil

Preheat oven to 475°. In the pan of a bread machine, combine warm water, olive oil, sugar and salt. Add flour to mixture and sprinkle with minced garlic and yeast. Select dough cycle and press Start. While dough is mixing, add oregano and basil. Let dough mix for 15 to 30 minutes. Remove dough and let stand for 5 to 30 minutes. The crust becomes thicker the longer it rests. On a lightly floured flat surface, roll out dough to fit desired pizza pan. Lightly grease pizza pan and spread dough evenly over the bottom. Add desired toppings and bake in oven for 12 to 15 minutes, or until golden brown.

Domino's Pizza is the world leader in home delivered pizza, with 7,000 stores in 46 international markets. In 2004, Domino's delivered 400 million pizzas.

Herbed Pizza Crust

Makes 1 (12") pizza crust

1 (1/4 oz.) pkg. active dry yeast	1/4 C. chopped herbs* 2 1/4 C. flour
1 tsp. sugar	1/2 tsp. salt
7 oz. warm water	1 T. garlic olive oil

Preheat oven to 425°. In a small mixing bowl, combine yeast, sugar and warm water. Let stand for 10 minutes, or until mixture is foamy. In a medium bowl, combine fresh chopped herbs. Add flour and salt and mix well. Add yeast mixture to flour mixture and continue to stir until dough forms a ball. Add garlic and olive oil and mix vigorously, until well combined. Place dough in a medium greased bowl and turn dough until it is well coated with oil. Cover bowl with a kitchen towel and set aside in a warm place for 1 hour, or until doubled in size. On a lightly floured flat surface, roll out dough. Place dough on a lightly greased pizza pan and top with desired ingredients. Bake in oven for 10 minutes, or until golden brown.

* Use various chopped herbs, such as: basil, thyme, parsley, oregano, rosemary or cilantro.

New York Style Pizza Crust

Makes 1 pizza crust

1/3 C. warm water	1/2 tsp. salt
1 tsp. active dry yeast	3 tsp. olive oil
3 C. bread flour, divided	

In a medium bowl, combine warm water and yeast, stirring gently until yeast is completely dissolved. Add 1 cup flour and salt, mixing well. Add another 1 cup flour and mix until dough forms a sticky ball. Sprinkle remaining 1 cup flour over a flat surface. Place dough on floured surface and knead until dough is smooth and no longer sticky. Lightly coat a large bowl with oil. Place dough in a bowl and turn dough until it is well coated with oil. Cover bowl with plastic wrap and set aside in a warm place for 45 minutes to 1 hour, or until doubled in size. Punch down dough and knead by hand for 2 to 3 minutes. Return dough to bowl and place in refrigerator for 15 minutes. Remove dough and stretch to desired size. Do not roll with a rolling pin. Place dough in a greased pizza pan and cover with desired toppings. Bake as desired.

Papa John's is often among the fastest growing franchises in America.

Quick and Crunchy Pizza Crust

Makes 1 pizza crust

2 C. flour
2 tsp. baking powder
Pinch of salt

1/4 C. olive oil
2/3 C. milk

   In a large bowl, combine flour, baking powder, salt, olive oil and milk. Mix thoroughly until well blended and mixture forms a dough. Roll out dough to desired size and place on a greased pizza pan or baking stone. Cover with desired toppings and bake as desired.

Of the roughly 31,386 pizza franchises in the United States, 83% offer delivery, 91% offer takeout and 51% offer dine-in service.

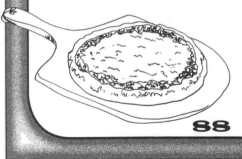

Thin Parmesan Pizza Crust

Makes 1 pizza crust

2/3 C. warm water
1 T. olive oil
1/4 tsp. salt
1/2 C. grated
   Parmesan cheese

2 C. bread flour
2 tsp. active dry yeast

   Preheat oven to 450°. Combine ingredients in bread machine pan as recommended by the bread machine manufacturer. Select dough cycle and press Start. When dough cycle has ended, remove dough from machine and knead on a lightly floured flat surface. Form dough into a tight ball, place in a greased bowl and let stand for 10 minutes. Remove from bowl and stretch dough to fit desired pizza pan. Place dough on a greased pizza pan and brush with additional olive oil. Cover pizza with desired toppings and bake in oven for 15 minutes, or until crust is golden brown.

   *Note: This dough may be refrigerated or frozen after resting for 10 minutes. Place in plastic bag that has been coated with cooking spray. Store in refrigerator for 7 to 10 days or freeze for up to 2 months. Thaw dough to room temperature before rolling out.

America's Basic Pizza Crust

Makes 2 pizza crusts

1 tsp. active dry yeast	2 T. Italian seasoning
1 tsp. sugar	1 tsp. salt
1/4 C. warm water	1 1/4 C. flat beer
4 C. bread flour	1 T. olive oil

In a small bowl, combine yeast, sugar and warm water. Mix lightly until yeast and sugar are completely dissolved and let stand for 10 minutes or until mixture is foamy. In a blender or food processor, combine flour, Italian seasoning and salt. Add yeast mixture, flat beer and olive oil and process until mixture forms a ball. Place dough ball on lightly floured surface and knead by hand until dough is elastic and smooth. Let dough rest for 2 to 3 minutes. Divide dough into 2 even balls. Place each dough ball into a separate bowl and cover with plastic wrap. Let rise for 1 hour at room temperature and store in refrigerator overnight. When ready for use, roll out dough to desired size and place over greased baking sheets. Cover with desired toppings and bake as desired.

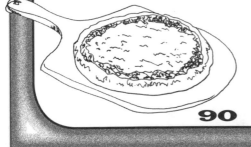

America's Basic Pizza Sauce

Makes about 3 cups

1/3 C. chopped onion
2 T. olive oil
2 T. minced garlic
1 (28 oz.) can Roma tomatoes in juice
2 (6 oz.) cans tomato paste

1 T. fresh chopped basil
1 T. fresh chopped parsley
1 tsp. fresh chopped oregano
1/2 tsp. pepper

In a large saucepan over medium heat, sauté chopped onion in olive oil, cooking until tender and transparent. Add minced garlic and sauté for 1 additional minute. Crush Roma tomatoes and add to mixture in saucepan with juice. Add tomato paste, chopped basil, chopped parsley, chopped oregano and pepper. Stir until well mixed and let simmer for 10 minutes. Spread sauce over pizza crust or place in an airtight container and chill in refrigerator or freezer until ready to use.

Each year, Las Vegas is home to the Pizza Expo, the world's largest pizza-only trade show.

Easy Herbed Pizza Sauce

Makes about 3 cups

**2 (14 1/2 oz.) cans
   whole peeled
   tomatoes in juice
1 (14 1/2 oz.) can
   pizza sauce**

**1/4 tsp. dried oregano
1/4 tsp. dried basil
1/4 tsp. dried marjoram
1/2 tsp. garlic salt
1/4 tsp. pepper**

In a large pot over medium heat, combine tomatoes in juice, pizza sauce, dried oregano, dried basil, dried marjoram, garlic salt and pepper. Let mixture simmer, reducing heat if needed, for 1 hour. Remove from heat and let sauce cool to room temperature. Spread sauce over pizza crust or place in an airtight container and chill in refrigerator or freezer until ready to use.

The Simple Sauce

Makes about 2 cups

**1 (15 oz.) can tomato
   sauce
1 (6 oz.) can tomato
   paste**

**1 T. dried oregano
1 1/2 tsp. minced garlic
1 tsp. paprika**

In a medium mixing bowl, combine tomato sauce and tomato paste, mixing until smooth. Stir in dried oregano, minced garlic and paprika. Mix well and spread sauce over pizza crust or place in an airtight container and chill in refrigerator or freezer until ready to use.

According to a recent Consumer Report on Eating Share Trends, pizza crusts rank as follows in preference:

Extra thin crust: 11%

Thin crust: 61%

Thick crust: 14%

Deep-dish crust: 14%

Crushed Tomato Sauce with Fennel Seeds

Makes 2 1/2 cups

1 clove garlic, minced
1 onion, chopped
1 T. olive oil
1 (28 oz.) can crushed
   tomatoes in juice
1/4 C. dry red or white
   wine

1/2 tsp. dried marjoram
1/2 tsp. dried oregano
1/2 tsp. dried basil
4 fennel seeds, crushed
1 small bay leaf
1/4 C. chopped chile
   peppers, optional

In a medium saucepan over medium heat, sauté minced garlic and onions in olive oil. Cook, stirring constantly, until onions are softened and transparent. Add crushed tomatoes in juice, wine, dried marjoram, dried oregano, dried basil, crushed fennel seeds, bay leaf and, if desired, chopped chile peppers. Bring mixture to a boil, stirring occasionally. Reduce heat and let simmer for 10 minutes. Remove bay leaf and spread sauce over pizza crust or place in an airtight container and chill in refrigerator or freezer until ready to use.

Fresh Italian Pizza Sauce

Makes 1 cup

2 ripe tomatoes, stems
   removed
1 clove garlic
1 T. fresh chopped basil
Pinch of cinnamon
1 tsp. salt

Pinch of pepper
1/4 tsp. sugar
1 tsp. dried oregano
2 T. olive oil
1 tsp. fresh chopped
   parsley

In a blender or food processor, combine tomatoes, garlic, chopped basil, cinnamon, salt, pepper, sugar, dried oregano, olive oil and chopped parsley. Process on high until mixture is blended with some chunks remaining. Spread sauce over pizza crust or place in an airtight container and chill in refrigerator or freezer until ready to use.

Each year in America, more pizzas are consumed during the week of the Super Bowl than another other week of the year.

95

Pizzeria Pizza Sauce

Makes about 2 cups

1 (6 oz.) can tomato
   paste
1 1/2 C. water
1/3 C. olive oil
2 cloves garlic, minced

Salt to taste
Pepper to taste
1/2 T. dried oregano
1/2 T. dried basil
1/2 tsp. dried rosemary

    In a large bowl, combine tomato paste, water and olive oil. Mix well and add minced garlic, salt, pepper, dried oregano, dried basil and dried rosemary. Mix until well combined, cover and let mixture stand for 3 hours to allow flavors to blend. Spread sauce over pizza crust or place in an airtight container and chill in refrigerator or freezer until ready to use.

Pesto Basil Pizza Sauce

Makes about 2 cups

12 walnuts, shelled
2 T. pine nuts
1 tsp. coarse salt
4 black peppercorns
3 cloves garlic
4 T. butter
3 C. dried basil

1/2 C. grated
Parmesan cheese
1/2 C. graded Romano
cheese
1 1/2 C. olive oil,
divided

In a blender or food processor, combine shelled walnuts, pine nuts, salt, peppercorns, garlic, butter, dried basil, grated Parmesan cheese, grated Romano cheese and 1/2 cup olive oil. Process on high until mixture is very fine. Add remaining 1 cup olive oil and process until sauce is very smooth. Spread sauce over pizza crust or place in an airtight container and chill in refrigerator or freezer until ready to use.

In the list of most popular food service items, pizza ranks second, only after burgers.

Olive & Anchovy Sauce

Makes about 1 cup

1/2 C. pitted black
    olives
1 clove garlic
1 1/2 T. capers

1 (2 oz.) can anchovies,
    drained
4 T. olive oil
Juice of 1 lemon

    In a blender or food processor, combine black olives, garlic, capers, drained anchovies, olive oil and lemon juice. Process on high until mixture is smooth. Spread mixture immediately over prepared pizza crust, cover with various toppings and bake as desired.

Among the older-than-50 market, pizza is the second most popular takeout food, after chicken.

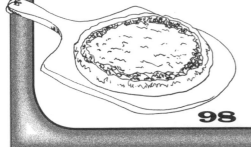

Garlic Lover's Pizza Sauce

Makes sauce for 2 pizzas

3 T. olive oil	1 (6 oz.) can tomato
1/2 C. minced onions	paste
1/2 C. minced green	1/2 tsp. dried basil
pepper	1/2 tsp. dried oregano
3 cloves garlic, minced	1 tsp. dried parsley
1 1/2 C. water	Salt and pepper, to taste

In a large deep skillet over medium high heat, combine olive oil, minced onions and minced green peppers, sautéing for about 5 minutes. Add minced garlic and continue to cook until onions and green peppers are tender. Slowly stir in water and tomato paste, mixing well. Add dried basil, dried oregano and dried parsley. Reduce heat and let simmer for 5 minutes. Add salt and pepper to taste and simmer, stirring often, for 30 minutes, or until sauce is thickened. Spread sauce over pizza crust or place in an airtight container and chill in refrigerator or freezer until ready to use.

Aioli Pizza Sauce

Makes 1 1/2 cups

2 cloves garlic, minced
2 egg yolks, room
   temperature
1 tsp. Dijon mustard
1 C. olive oil, room
   temperature

2 tsp. fresh lemon juice
Salt and pepper, to
   taste, optional

In a large bowl, combine minced garlic, egg yolks and Dijon mustard. Using a wire whisk, mix well until thickened, adding olive oil as necessary. Mixture should become thick and creamy after about 1/2 cup of the oil has been added. Slowly pour remaining 1/2 cup oil into mixture and add lemon juice. If desired, season with salt and pepper to taste. Spread mixture immediately over prepared pizza crust, cover with various toppings and bake as desired. Or, if desired, refrigerate sauce for up to 5 days.

In Taiwan, the top selling pizza is a seafood delight, containing onions, peas, squid, shrimp and crab.

100

Dessert Pizza

Banana Cream Dessert Pizza

Makes 1 (12") pizza

1 (12") pre-baked
   pizza crust
2/3 C. brown sugar
1/4 C. butter, softened
1/3 C. chopped pecans
1 (3 oz.) pkg. instant
   banana pudding mix

4 bananas, sliced
1 C. whipped topping
English toffee bits for
   garnish

Preheat oven to 350°. On a large baking sheet or pizza pan, place the pizza crust. In a small bowl, mix together brown sugar, softened butter and chopped pecans. Sprinkle the mixture evenly over the crust. Bake in oven for 15 minutes, remove and let cool completely. Prepare pudding according to package directions and refrigerate until ready to assemble. Spread banana slices evenly over the crust and cover with prepared pudding. Top with whipped cream and sprinkles of toffee bits. Chill in refrigerator until ready to serve.

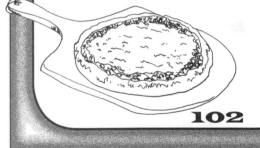

Easy Fudge Pizza Pie

Makes 1 (12") pizza

1 (12") pre-baked pizza crust	1 tsp. flour
1/4 C. plus 2 tsp. butter, melted, divided	3/4 C. sugar
	1 egg, beaten
	1/4 C. evaporated milk
3 T. cocoa powder	1 tsp. vanilla
	Whipped topping

Preheat oven to 400°. Line a pizza pan or baking sheet with parchment paper trimmed so that edges do not hang over. Place pizza crust on pan and brush 2 teaspoons melted butter over crust and rim. Set aside. In a small bowl combine cocoa powder, flour and sugar. Mix well and set aside. In a medium bowl, combine beaten egg, remaining 1/4 cup melted butter, evaporated milk and vanilla, stirring well. Add the cocoa mixture to the egg mixture. Stir well and pour over the crust. Bake in oven for 15 minutes, remove and let cool. Slice and serve with a dollop of whipped topping.

In Greece, the Hellenic is a popular pizza, which has pepperoni, onions, green peppers, fresh tomatoes, Greek olives, feta cheese and oregano.

Caramel Apple Dessert Pizza

Makes 1 (12") pizza

1 (20 oz.) pkg.
   refrigerated sugar
   cookie dough
1 (8 oz.) pkg. cream
   cheese, softened
1/4 C. creamy
   peanut butter
1/2 C. brown sugar

1/2 tsp. vanilla
2 Granny Smith apples,
   peeled and sliced
1 C. lemon-lime soda
Cinnamon, to taste
1/4 C. caramel topping
1/2 C. chopped
   peanuts, optional

Preheat oven to 350°. Press sugar cookie dough firmly and evenly into a greased 12" pizza pan. Bake in oven for 20 minutes, or until golden brown. Remove and let cool on a wire rack. In a medium bowl, combine softened cream cheese, peanut butter, brown sugar and vanilla, mixing until smooth. Spread mixture over cookie dough in pan. To prevent browning, dip apple slices in lemon-lime soda and arrange apple slices on top of the cream cheese spread. Sprinkle lightly with cinnamon. Heat caramel topping slightly in microwave and drizzle over apples. If desired, top with chopped peanuts.

Cheesecake Cookie Pizza á la Raspberry

Makes 12 to 16 servings

3/4 C. butter or
   margarine, softened
3/4 C. plus 1 T. sugar,
   divided
1 egg yolk
1 tsp. vanilla
1 1/2 C. flour, divided

1 (8 oz.) pkg. cream
   cheese, softened
1 egg
1/3 C. raspberry
   preserves
1/4 C. sliced almonds,
   toasted

Preheat oven to 350°. To make dough, in a large mixing bowl, beat the butter at medium to high speed for 30 seconds. Add 3/4 cup sugar and continue to beat well. Add egg yolk and vanilla, beating until well combined. Gradually add 1 cup flour, beating with the mixer. Add remaining flour and mix with a wooden spoon. In a lightly greased pizza pan, spread dough and bake in oven for approximately 25 minutes, or until golden brown. In another large mixing bowl, combine softened cream cheese, egg and remaining 1 tablespoon sugar, beating until smooth. Spread cream cheese mixture over the hot crust, to within 1/2" of the edge. Place dollops of raspberry preserves on top. Gently swirl preserves with a knife to marble the topping. Sprinkle with sliced almonds. Bake in oven for an additional 5 to 10 minutes, or until filling is set. Let cool before cutting into pieces. Store leftovers in refrigerator.

Dessert Oreo Pizza

Makes 1 (14") pizza

1 (21 oz.) pkg.
  brownie mix
1 1/2 C. Oreo cookie
  crumbs
1 C. miniature
  marshmallows

1/4 C. chopped walnuts
1/4 C. Reese's Pieces
  peanut butter candies

Preheat oven to 350°. Lightly coat a 14" deep-dish pizza pan with cooking spray and set aside. Prepare brownie mix according to package directions. Stir in cookie crumbs. Mix well and spread mixture over prepared pan. Bake in oven for 18 minutes, until a toothpick inserted in center of brownies comes out clean. Sprinkle marshmallows evenly over hot brownies and return to oven for an additional 3 minutes, until marshmallows are lightly browned. Sprinkle with chopped walnuts and peanut butter candies. Press candies and walnuts gently into marshmallows. Cut into squares and serve warm.

Blueberry Dessert Pizza

Makes 1 (12") pizza

1 (18 oz.) pkg. white
    cake mix
1 1/4 C. quick oats,
    divided
1/2 C. butter or
    margarine,
    softened, divided

1 egg
1/2 C. chopped nuts
1/4 C. brown sugar
1/2 tsp. cinnamon
1 (21 oz.) can
    blueberry fruit filling

Preheat oven to 350°. Grease a 12" pizza pan and set aside. In a large mixing bowl, combine cake mix, 1 cup quick oats and 6 tablespoons butter, beating at low speed until mixture is crumbly. Set aside 1 cup crumbs for topping. Add egg to the remaining crumbs. Mix well and press mixture in prepared pizza pan. Bake in oven for 12 minutes. In the same bowl, combine remaining 1/4 cup oats, remaining 2 tablespoons butter, chopped nuts, brown sugar, cinnamon and 1 cup reserved crumb topping. Remove crust from oven and spread blueberry filling evenly over hot crust and sprinkle crumb mixture over top. Return to oven an additional 15 to 20 minutes, or until topping is golden brown. Let cool completely before cutting into wedges and serving.

Fresh Peach Pizza

Makes 1 (12") pizza

1/2 C. butter, softened	1/2 C. orange juice
1/4 C. powdered sugar	1/2 C. red currant jelly
1 C. flour	5 C. sliced fresh peaches
1 T. cornstarch	Whipped topping
2 T. sugar	

Preheat oven to 350°. In a medium bowl, cream together butter and powdered sugar. Stir in flour and mix well. Press mixture into a 12" pizza pan and prick with a fork. Bake in oven for 10 minutes, until lightly browned. To make filling, in a double boiler over medium heat, combine cornstarch and sugar, mixing well. Stir in orange juice and currant jelly. Heat mixture, stirring constantly, until mixture begins to boil and thickens. Remove from heat and let cool. Arrange sliced peaches over crust and gently pour sauce mixture evenly over peaches. Chill in refrigerator until glaze is set. Serve with whipped topping.

In the U.K., the most popular pizza is named the Full House and has onions, green peppers, ham, spicy beef, sausage, sweet corn and pineapple.

Cookie Pizza
with Pralines

Makes 1 (12") pizza

**3/4 C. butter or
   margarine, softened**
**1 C. brown sugar,
   divided**
1 egg yolk
**1 1/2 tsp. vanilla,
   divided**

1 1/2 C. flour
3/4 C. sour cream
**16 pecan halves,
   toasted***
**1/2 C. chopped
   pecans, toasted***

Preheat oven to 350°. To make dough, in a large mixing bowl, beat butter for 30 seconds at medium to high speed. Add 3/4 cup brown sugar and beat well. Add egg yolk and 1 teaspoon vanilla, beating until well combined. Gradually add 1 cup flour, beating with mixer. Stir in remaining flour with a wooden spoon. Lightly grease a 12" pizza pan. Spread dough on bottom and up edge of prepared pan. Bake in oven for 20 minutes, or until golden brown. In a small bowl, combine sour cream, remaining 1/4 cup brown sugar and remaining 1/2 teaspoon vanilla. Spread mixture over hot crust to within 1/2" of the edge. Place pecan halves around the edge of the pizza crust and sprinkle chopped pecans over remaining pizza. Let cool at room temperature allowing topping to set. Store leftovers in refrigerator.

*To toast, place walnut halves and chopped walnuts in a single layer on two separate baking sheets. Bake at 350° for approximately 10 minutes or until walnuts are golden brown.

Fruit & Brownie Pizza

Makes 1 (12") pizza

1/2 C. margarine,
   softened
1 3/4 C. sugar, divided
4 eggs, divided
2 tsp. vanilla, divided
1 C. flour

3/4 C. cocoa powder
1 (8 oz.) pkg. cream
   cheese, softened
2 C. assorted fresh
   sliced fruits

Preheat oven to 350°. In a large bowl, combine margarine and 1 1/2 cups sugar, mixing at medium speed until fluffy. Blend in 3 eggs and 1 teaspoon vanilla. Add flour and cocoa powder, mixing well. Spread batter on a lightly greased 12" pizza pan. Bake in oven for 15 minutes. In a medium mixing bowl, beat cream cheese until smooth. Add remaining 1/4 cup sugar, remaining 1 egg and remaining 1 teaspoon vanilla and spread over baked brownie crust. Return to oven for an additional 15 minutes. Remove from oven and let cool. Once brownie pizza has cooled, top with assorted fresh sliced fruits.

Simple Strawberry Pizza

Makes 1 (12") pizza

1 (20 oz.) pkg.
   refrigerated sugar
   cookie dough
1 (8 oz.) pkg. cream
   cheese, softened

1/3 C. sugar
1 (8 oz.) tub whipped
   topping
2 C. sliced strawberries

Preheat oven to 350°. Grease a 12" pizza pan. Press sugar cookie dough firmly into pan and bake in oven for 20 minutes, or until golden brown. In a large mixing bowl, beat together cream cheese and sugar until smooth. Gently fold in whipped topping. Spread cream cheese mixture over cooled pizza crust. Arrange sliced strawberries evenly over top. Chill in refrigerator until ready to serve.

Domino's Ranchera Pizza with frijoles, onions, jalapenos, chorizo and extra cheese is popular in Mexico.

Oatmeal Cookie Pizza

Makes 1 (12") pizza

3/4 C. flour
3/4 C. old fashioned oats
1/2 tsp. baking powder
1/4 tsp. baking soda
1/3 C. butter, softened
1/3 C. sugar

1/3 C. brown sugar
1 egg
1 tsp. vanilla
Chocolate chips, raisins
   or nuts, optional

Preheat oven to 375°. In a large bowl, combine flour, oats, baking powder and baking soda. In a separate large bowl, combine butter, sugar, brown sugar, egg and vanilla, mixing until well blended. Gradually add the oats mixture to the sugar mixture, stirring until well blended. Lightly grease a 12" pizza pan and press the mixture evenly into the bottom. If desired, press chocolate chips, raisins or nuts into the dough. Bake in oven for 12 to 15 minutes, or until lightly browned. Remove from oven and let cool for 10 to 15 minutes. To serve, loosen with a spatula and cut into pieces.

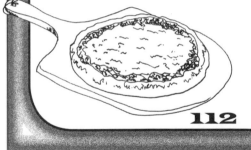

Chocolate Frosted Cookie Pizza

Makes 1 (12") pizza

1/2 C. plus 2 T. butter,
    divided
1/2 C. brown sugar
1/4 C. sugar
1 tsp. vanilla
1 egg
1 1/4 C. flour
1/2 tsp. baking soda

6 oz. chocolate chips
3 T. milk
1 C. powdered sugar
1/2 C. pecan halves
1/2 C. M & M's
1/4 C. shredded coconut
2 oz. white chocolate,
    melted

Preheat oven to 350˚. In a large bowl, combine 1/2 cup butter, brown sugar, sugar, vanilla and egg, mixing until well blended. Gradually stir in flour and baking soda, stirring until dough is stiff. Press dough evenly into an ungreased 12" pizza pan. Bake in oven for 15 minutes, or until golden brown. Remove from oven and let cool. In a medium saucepan over low heat, combine chocolate chips, remaining 2 tablespoons butter and milk. Remove from heat and stir in powdered sugar until smooth and ready to spread. If necessary, add a few drops of hot water to make the frosting glossy. Spread frosting evenly over the cooled cookie. Immediately sprinkle with pecan halves, M&M's and shredded coconut, pressing toppings lightly into the frosting. Drizzle melted white chocolate over cookie and let stand until hardened.

Nutty Coconut Pizza

Makes 2 (10") pizzas

1 1/2 C. flour
2 tsp. baking soda
1 tsp. salt
2 1/3 C. old
    fashioned oats
1 C. butter, softened
1 1/2 C. brown sugar
2 eggs

1/2 tsp. vanilla
1 1/2 C. shredded
    coconut, divided
1/2 C chopped walnuts
2 C. chocolate chips
1 C. M&M's
1 C. peanuts

Preheat oven to 350°. In a large bowl combine flour, baking soda, salt and oats, stirring until well blended. In a separate large bowl, cream together butter, brown sugar, eggs and vanilla. Add creamed mixture to flour mixture, stirring well. Mix in 1/2 cup shredded coconut and chopped walnuts. Grease two 10" pizza pans. Divide dough into 2 sections and spread evenly over bottom of each pan. Bake in oven for 10 minutes. Remove pizza crust from oven and let cool. Sprinkle chocolate chips, remaining 1 cup shredded coconut, M&M's and peanuts over top of pizza. Return to oven for an additional 5 to 10 minutes, or until golden brown. Remove from oven and cool on wire racks before serving.

Banana Split Supreme Dessert Pizza

Makes 1 (12") pizza

1 (12") pre-baked
    pizza crust
1 T. butter, melted
1 C. milk
1/4 tsp. vanilla
1 1/3 C. chocolate chips
3 bananas, sliced
    1/4" thick lengthwise

1 (8 oz.) can crushed
    pineapple, drained
1/2 C. strawberry
    preserves
2 C. thinly sliced
    strawberries
Whipped topping

Preheat oven to 400°. Brush pizza crust, including rim, with melted butter before placing directly on oven rack. Bake in oven for 5 minutes, remove and let cool. In a glass measuring cup, heat milk in microwave. In a blender or food processor, combine hot milk, vanilla and chocolate chips, blending until smooth. Refrigerate mixture for 1 1/2 hours or until slightly thickened. Place sliced bananas evenly over pizza crust. Sprinkle with drained pineapple and spread strawberry preserves evenly over top of the pizza. Stir chilled chocolate mixture before pouring over strawberry preserves. Place in refrigerator for 1 hour. Before serving, arrange strawberry slices over chocolate filling and garnish with whipped topping.

Ricotta Carmel Apple Pizza

Make 1 (12") pizza

1 (12") pre-baked pizza crust	3 T. sugar
1 T. butter, softened	1/2 tsp. cinnamon
1 (15 oz.) container ricotta cheese	1 (20 oz.) can apple fruit filling
1/3 C. heavy whipping cream	1 (8 oz.) container whipped topping
	3/4 C. caramel topping

Preheat oven to 400°. Place pizza crust on a 12" pizza pan or baking sheet. Brush butter over the pizza crust and rim. Bake in oven for 5 minutes, remove and let cool on a wire rack. In a large mixing bowl, combine ricotta cheese, heavy cream, sugar and cinnamon. Beat for 3 minutes at high speed. Spread mixture evenly over pizza crust and top with apple fruit filling. Garnish with whipped topping and drizzle with caramel topping.

Gourmet Almond Chocolate Pizza

Makes 1 (12") pizza

1 (12") pre-baked pizza crust	1 (12 oz.) bag chocolate chips
4 T. sugar	1/4 C. sliced almonds
4 T. butter, melted	Powdered sugar, optional

Preheat oven to 400°. Place pizza crust on a 12" pizza pan that has been lined with parchment paper. In a double boiler over medium low heat, slowly melt sugar and butter, stirring constantly. Spread mixture evenly over the entire pizza crust. Bake in oven for 10 minutes, or until butter mixture turns golden in color. Remove from oven and immediately sprinkle with chocolate chips. Let stand for 2 minutes or until chips are melted enough to spread. Spread chocolate evenly over the crust and gently press almonds into the chocolate. If desired, sprinkle powdered sugar over chocolate. Chill in refrigerator for 15 minutes before serving.

Neapolitan Pizza

Makes 1 (12") pizza

1 (12") pre-baked pizza crust	1 1/2 C. powdered sugar

1/4 C. plus 4 T. butter,
   softened, divided
	3 C. chocolate chips
	1 C. heavy whipping
	   cream

1 (8 oz.) pkg. cream cheese	3/4 tsp. cinnamon 3 C. sliced strawberries
5 tsp. vanilla, divided	1 C. walnuts, toasted*

Preheat oven to 350°. Place pizza crust on a 12" pizza pan or baking sheet. Brush 1 tablespoon butter evenly over crust. Bake in oven for 9 minutes, remove and let cool on a wire rack. In a medium mixing bowl, beat cream cheese, 1/4 cup butter, 1 teaspoon vanilla and powdered sugar at medium speed. Set aside. In a double boiler over medium heat, melt chocolate chips, heavy cream, remaining 4 tablespoons butter, cinnamon and remaining 4 teaspoons vanilla. Stir until well blended. Remove from heat and let cool slightly. Spread cream cheese mixture evenly over crust and place sliced strawberries evenly on top. Drizzle the melted chocolate mixture generously over the strawberries and top with toasted walnuts.

*To toast, place walnuts in a single layer on a baking sheet. Bake at 350° for approximately 10 minutes or until walnuts are golden brown.

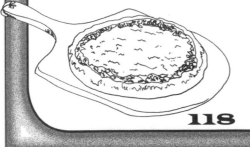

Index

Breakfast Pizza

Breakfast Pizza Casserole 6
Cheesy Tomato & Mushroom Breakfast Pizza 9
Croissant Sausage Breakfast Pizza 7
Double Sausage Breakfast Pie 10
Egg & Ham Biscuit Pizzas.................................... 4
Gourmet Smoked Salmon Breakfast Pizza 3
Pizza Omelet 5
Pizza Pancakes.. 8
Ricotta Pizza Quiche....................................... 12
Sausage & Egg Breakfast Pizza.............................. 2
Sweet Apple Cheddar Breakfast Pizza................... 11

Appetizer Party Pizza

Apple Pizza Pie.. 23
Brie Pecan Party Pizza 24
Broccoli Ranch Veggie Pizza 19
Cheese-Stuffed Pizza Puffs.................................. 21
Easy Pizza Logs.. 22
Gelatin Fruit Pizza.. 20
Hot Dog Pizza 27
Italian Pizza Roll Bread...................................... 26
No-Bake Chicken Veggie Pizza 14
Party Pizzas on Rye... 17
Pizza Roll-Ups 15
Strawberry Almond Pizza.................................... 28
Sugar Cookie Fruit Pizza 25
Three Cheese Pizza Wedges 18
Veggie Pizza Bites... 16

Main Dish Pizza

Alfredo Crab Pizza 44
Basic Grilled Pizza 62
BBQ Chicken Pizza.. 51
BLT Pizza.. 30
Buffalo Chicken Pizza 57
Chicken Caesar Salad Pizza............................. 32
Chicken Enchilada Pizza 60
Easy Three Cheese Pepperoni Pizza................. 59
Fajita Pizza... 37
Feta, Onions & Spinach Pizza 39
Four Cheese Pizza 40
Garlic Veggie Chicken Pizza............................. 36
Gourmet Chicken Pizza.................................... 46
Grilled Meat 'n Veggie Pizza 54
Grilled Onion Ranch Pizza 55
Hawaiian BBQ Chicken Pizza 56
Herbed White Pizza... 35
Meatball Pizza.. 52
Mexican Pizza 50
No-Sauce Veggie Pizza Pie 41
Pepperoni Stuffed-Crust Pizza 49
Philly Cheese Steak Pizza 42
Pineapple Teriyaki Chicken Pizza...................... 47
Potato Bacon Pizza 53
Simple Artichoke Pesto Pizza........................... 38
Simple Pesto Pizza Pie.................................... 61
Smoked Salmon Pizza 33
Spaghetti Pizza Pie 45
Thai Chicken & Shrimp Pizza 31
Tropical Shrimp Pizza 43
Upside Down Pizza 48
Vegetables Florentine Pizza............................. 58
Zucchini Crust Pizza.. 34

Pizza for One

Apple & Feta Pan Pizzas.................................. 77
Cheeseburger Pizzas...................................... 73
Easy Pita Pizzas 74
Grilled Pizza Wraps 69
Hawaiian Pita Pizza....................................... 75
Hearty Chili Pizzas.. 65
Italian Sausage & Pineapple Pizzas 78
Mexican Chicken Pizzas 71
Mini Bagel Bites 72
Mini Pizza Rounds... 76
Pepperoni Mushroom Calzones 67
Pizza Pot Pies.. 66
Pizzas with Goat Cheese & Red Peppers........... 64
Red Pepper Pizza Grilled Sandwiches............... 70
Spinach Artichoke Calzones 68

Crusts and Sauces

Aioli Pizza Sauce 100
America's Basic Pizza Crust........................... 90
America's Basic Pizza Sauce........................... 91
Basic Pizza Crust.. 80
Bread Machine Garlic Pizza Crust 84
Crushed Tomato Sauce with Fennel Seeds......... 94
Easy Herbed Pizza Sauce............................... 92
Fresh Italian Pizza Sauce............................... 95
Garlic Lover's Pizza Sauce.............................. 99
Herbed Pizza Crust 86
Italian Pizza Crust 85
New York Style Pizza Crust 87
Olive & Anchovy Sauce 98
Pesto Basil Pizza Sauce 97
Pizza Shop Pizza Crust 82

Pizzeria Pizza Sauce.. 96
Quick and Crunchy Pizza Crust 88
Soft-on-the-Inside Pizza Crust........................ 81
Sweet Whole Wheat Pizza Crust 83
The Simple Sauce.. 93
Thin Parmesan Pizza Crust............................. 89

Dessert Pizza

Banana Cream Dessert Pizza...........................102
Banana Split Supreme Dessert Pizza 115
Blueberry Desert Pizza 107
Easy Fudge Pizza Pie.....................................103
Caramel Apple Dessert Pizza..........................104
Cheesecake Cookie Pizza á la Raspberry 105
Chocolate Frosted Cookie Pizza 113
Cookie Pizza with Pralines.............................109
Dessert Oreo Pizza 106
Fresh Peach Pizza 108
Fruit & Brownie Pizza 110
Gourmet Almond Chocolate Pizza 117
Neapolitan Pizza...118
Nutty Coconut Pizza......................................114
Oatmeal Cookie Pizza....................................112
Ricotta Carmel Apple Pizza 116
Simple Strawberry Pizza................................111

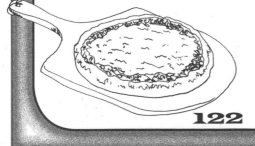